SAGE
ADVICE

The Lives and Maxims of
Some of History's Wisest People

Richard K. Borden

Publishing services provided by  **Archangel Ink**

ISBN: 978-1-950043-23-1

To my parents for showing me how to live a flourishing life; and to my wife and children for allowing me to experience the joy of family.

Contents

PREFACE

For more than 200,000 years, people have looked to religion, philosophy, and the example of their ancestors for guidance on how to live their lives. The need for common rules and guiding ideals grew especially important after the development of agriculture 10,000 years ago, which led to the increasingly crowded, complex, and interdependent planet we live on today. Successful people and cultures from across the world and throughout time have independently developed common rules of behavior that have allowed them to flourish. Those individuals, families, and societies that follow these natural laws have been more likely to thrive throughout history.

Today, however, many people have grown disillusioned with the religious, philosophical, and historical traditions that successfully guided our ancestors for millennia. Some ignore the noble truths at the heart of the world's great religions because they are distracted by each creed's inconsistencies with modern science and their sometimes fanciful theologies. Ancient philosophies may be seen as having no relevance to the modern world, and good advice from our ancestors may be dismissed as trite platitudes rather than embraced as the expression of timeless truths. Some people may also choose to ignore the wisdom of great historical figures because they remove these men and women from their historical context, judging them instead against today's ephemeral cultural obsessions and rejecting everything if they are found deficient in anything. This has led to a void in modern culture that is often filled with hedonism, moral relativism, wishful thinking, and shallow ideas that are unlikely to withstand the uncompromising test of time. As the strength of traditional religion fades and as the proven philosophical wisdom of our ancestors is ignored by modern societies, what is to take its place?

Instead of looking at the distinctive flaws of the world's different

1

religions, philosophical traditions, and great historic figures, it is more enlightening to look at their common strengths and insights. As Aristotle said, "We are all flawed in unique ways but good in only one way."[1] This book attempts to lay out the common wisdom of some of history's great thinkers and to help illuminate the "Way," which is common to most successful people and cultures. These are great philosophers, scientists, artists, statesmen, and saints whose words and deeds call to us from the past. The wisdom and the extraordinary lives of these sages illustrate the key virtues necessary to live a happy and flourishing life—not just for yourself, but for your family, your friends, your descendants, and your country. These precepts have not only been proven through the course of human history but are also increasingly supported by the findings of modern neuroscience, genetics, psychology, and economics. I have been inspired to be a better person through my study of these common ideals, and I plot my life's course with more confidence when following in the footsteps of history's great men and women.

---

1 Aristotle, *Aristotle's Nicomachean Ethics*, translated by R.C. Bartlett and S.D. Collins (Chicago: University of Chicago Press, 2011).

INTRODUCTION

This book contains the wisdom of eighteen of history's great sages. From the ancient world: Ptah-Hotep of Egypt; Confucius of China; Buddha of India; Aristotle of Greece; Seneca, Jesus, and Marcus Aurelius of Imperial Rome; and Muhammad of Arabia. From the early modern world: Zhu Xi of Song Dynasty China; Elizabeth Tudor of Renaissance England; Benjamin Franklin and George Washington of America's founding generation; Catherine the Great of eighteenth-century Russia, and Johann Wolfgang von Goethe from nineteenth-century Germany. Lastly, from the twentieth century: Theodore Roosevelt and George Washington Carver of the United States, Mahatma Gandhi of India, and Winston Churchill of the United Kingdom.

The words and examples of these eighteen sages span more than four thousand years of human history and cross the globe (Figures 1 and 2). Despite the great separation in time, space, and culture, their teachings are remarkably consistent. I believe each person has perceived and transmitted natural laws that are universal and applicable to almost all successful people and societies. These laws are generally self-evident, and no single society, religion, or individual has had a monopoly on such wisdom. As Cicero, the great Roman statesman and philosopher of the first century BCE, wrote in his influential work *De Republica (On the Republic)*, "There is a true law, right reason in accord with nature, it is of universal application, unchanging and eternal; its commands urge us to do our duty and its prohibitions restrain us from doing evil.... It is wrong to abrogate this law and it cannot be annulled.... There is one law eternal and unchangeable, binding at all times upon all nations."[2] I leave it to the reader to decide whether

---

2   Marcus Tullius Cicero, *De Republica*, translated by Francis Barham (London: Edmund Spettigue, 1841).

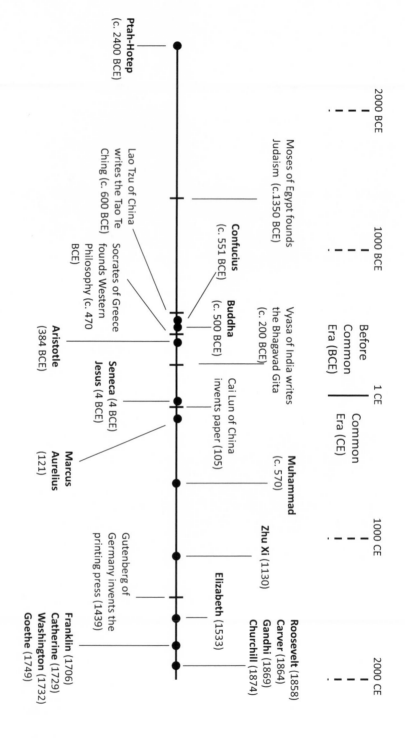

Figure 1 – Historical Context

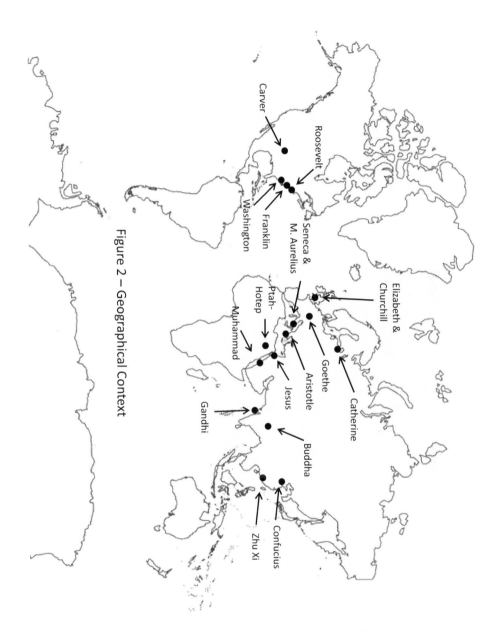

Figure 2 – Geographical Context

these natural laws are a gift transmitted by God, a genetic blueprint created by millions of years of human and prehuman evolution, and/ or rules that successful societies and individuals have lived by and transmitted to their descendants, while their unsuccessful counterparts have failed and passed into oblivion.

This book is organized into four broad sections: 1) an introduction that describes why these particular individuals were selected from among the thousands of extraordinary people in human history; 2) an effort to place each person within their global historical and cultural context; 3) a series of brief biographies to provide the reader with an understanding of each person's life and character; and, finally, 4) a collection of their selected quotes organized by subject. This book does not need to be read in order. In fact, I encourage you to skip directly to the biographies or quotes if you wish. It is easy to return to an earlier section if you want to learn more about the person or the context from which the quote was taken.

The quotes of these eighteen people are presented in a brief, easily understood, and memorable form known as the maxim. A *maxim* is a short statement of a fundamental principle, truth, or rule for living. Maxims have been popular throughout human history and across all cultures. They form the core of *The Analects of Confucius*, the book of Proverbs in the Bible, in the writings of Seneca, and in the Hadith (quotes) of the Prophet Muhammad. One of the first international best sellers after the invention of the printing press was a collection of classical maxims by the Dutch scholar Erasmus in the early 1500s. The earliest surviving writing of George Washington is a recopying of a collection of 110 maxims called the "Rules of Civility and Decent Behavior." Maxims were also a centerpiece of Ben Franklin's *Poor Richard's Almanack*. The maxim continues to be a popular form in modern times, often presented as collected quotes from great figures such as Albert Einstein, Nelson Mandela, and Lee Kuan Yew. The maxims have been grouped by subject for ease of reference and to allow the reader to better compare and contrast each sage's advice. By necessity, some topics have many more entries than others because subjects such as religion or honesty were much more commonly spoken or written about compared to more prosaic but still important topics such as humor.

Six of these sages spoke and wrote almost exclusively in English, while Gandhi communicated in both English and several of India's native tongues. The maxims of Queen Elizabeth, Franklin, Washington, Roosevelt, Carver, Churchill, and Gandhi are presented verbatim. Although some of the wording in these maxims may sound archaic to modern ears, the meaning is still easily grasped. Maxims from these English speakers were only sourced from credible and carefully researched compilations or from multiple sources to avoid falsely attributing a saying to them.

The words of the other sages all require translation into modern English. This introduces an element of uncertainty and personal interpretation into the final wording. The maxims of Ptah-Hotep, Confucius, Buddha, Aristotle, Seneca, Marcus Aurelius, Muhammad, and Goethe are based on at least three independent translations into English. Using the different translations as guides, I have tried to capture the core truth of the maxim in simple modern English. By necessity, many of the maxims of Zhu Xi and Catherine are based on only a single translation because of the limited availability of their works in English. Translations from the Koran must be approached carefully because, according to Islamic tradition, these words come directly from God, have existed forever, and were dictated directly in Arabic from God to humans via Muhammad. In acknowledgment of these sensitivities, the Muhammad quotes in this book are based on three translations by renowned and sympathetic scholars of the Koran. Careful translation of Jesus's words is also required because many Christians believe in the divine inspiration of the Bible, and multiple translations have been required to arrive at an English language version of his teachings. Jesus likely preached in the Aramaic language, but his words were first written down in ancient Greek before eventually being translated into English. Any quotes from Jesus are simply copied verbatim from the New International Version of the Bible because of these complexities.

There have been many wise men and women scattered throughout human history, so narrowing the group to these eighteen was a difficult exercise. Key to the decision were 1) they all created a large body of quotes and writings on a broad variety of topics that have survived to the present day, 2) the great majority of their teachings offer good advice, 3) they led admirable lives and were good teachers, and 4) they represent the best of many different cultures and historical eras.

There are only two women in this group, not because of lesser wisdom or insight, but because, for most of human history and in almost all cultures, few women were allowed the opportunity to fully express themselves. Queen Elizabeth I and Catherine the Great are historical exceptions because they were prolific writers and wisely wielded great power and influence during a time when women typically had far fewer rights and opportunities. It is perhaps no coincidence that both of these women were from northern Europe. Even the Roman historian Tacitus, writing two thousand years ago, observed that the barbarian women beyond the empire's northern frontier shared many rights and responsibilities with their husbands and that "she comes as the man's partner in toils and dangers; and in both peace and in war she is to share in his suffering and adventures."[3] It is only in recent history and predominantly in Europe and its cultural transplants that near equality of the genders has been attained, while women's rights are still severely restricted in the Islamic world. In the interests of consistency with the original text, I have left the masculine nouns and pronouns within most of the quotes. However, despite the

---

3   Publius Cornelius Tacitus, *The Germania*, translated by A.J. Church and W.J. Brodribb (London: MacMillan and Company, 1868).

preponderance of male authors quoted in this book, I believe that almost all of the advice provided is equally applicable to both men and women.

Of course, to be quoted, a person's words must still be accessible to us either through their own writings or the writings of their followers and observers. There are many outstanding men and women who have led noble and inspiring lives; however, few such people have also created a significant written record of their insights about life. There are also many ancient authors who might have offered great wisdom but whose works have been lost. Before the invention of paper in China was linked with the invention of the movable type printing press in Germany, almost all written works had to be laboriously hand-copied onto expensive parchment, cumbersome clay tablets, or fragile papyrus. There were few copies of even the most famous works in existence, and these were easily lost through war, fire, censorship, or neglect. Similarly, regions with rich oral traditions but with few surviving written works, such as pre-colonial sub-Saharan Africa or pre-Columbian America, may appear underrepresented.

Each of these sages has said things that I personally disagree with, but in general their good advice vastly outweighs the bad. Conversely, there are many people who have created one or a handful of noble maxims but have also offered much bad advice in other areas. Even the most brutal despots of the twentieth century (Joseph Stalin, Adolf Hitler, and Mao Zedong) said and wrote some noble things. Much like Moses of the Jewish Torah and Christian Old Testament, Muhammad falls in between these two extremes. Both the Koran and the Old Testament of the Bible do indeed contain much good and principled advice. However, this good counsel is sometimes overshadowed by the many statements made against unbelievers that can be used to justify intolerance, oppression, and violence toward people of other faiths, nations, or opinions. This collection only includes carefully selected quotes from the Koran that are consistent with living an ethical, just, and appropriately tolerant life.

As Seneca wrote, "Think about the benefit that good example provides us, and you will realize that great men's presence and their memory are both useful."[4] I believe a sage must be more than merely a good teacher; their lives should also show the practical outcomes of their beliefs and principles. This applies to both their public and personal lives, which I consider equally important to demonstrate character. History is filled with religious, philosophical, and political hypocrites whose words and actions imply that their advice applies to everyone except themselves. As Benjamin Franklin stated, "Well done is better than well said."[5]

I have also tried to select individuals who represent the best of different cultures, religions, and time periods. In part, this is to capture the unique wisdom of different cultures, but more importantly to show their striking similarities. All of the world's current most populous religions are represented here in the words of the founders of Confucianism, Buddhism, Christianity, and Islam, while Hinduism is represented by its most famous modern-day exemplar, Mahatma Gandhi. Of the eighteen, only Benjamin Franklin and George Washington lived in the same time and place and knew each other well.

Many of these people had a profound influence on the course of human events. In fact, over half of the eighteen (Confucius, Buddha, Aristotle, Jesus, Muhammad, Elizabeth, Franklin, Washington, Gandhi, and Churchill) are routinely ranked among the one hundred most influential people in human history.[6,7] However, this is

---

4   Moses Hadas, *The Stoic Philosophy of Seneca: Essays and Letters* (New York: Norton and Company, 1958).

5   Benjamin Franklin, *Wit and Wisdom from Poor Richard's Almanack* (New York: Dover Publications, 1999).

6   *The 100 Most Influential People of all Time, Time Magazine* (New York: Time Books, 2012).

7   Michael Hart, *The 100: A Ranking of the Most Influential Persons in History* (New York: Citadel Press, 1994).

largely incidental and was not a selection criteria for inclusion in this book. Being highly influential sometimes requires a single-minded pursuit of a narrow goal and does not necessarily guarantee someone will be a source of broad advice for the rest of us.

THE SAGES IN HISTORICAL
AND RELIGIOUS CONTEXT

Ptah-Hotep, Confucius, and Buddha were almost certainly unknown to each other and developed their maxims in complete independence. Aristotle may also have been unaware of the writings of the three earlier men. However, the sages who lived in later periods would have been more clearly influenced by the teachings of those who came before them. Ptah-Hotep and the long Egyptian tradition of wisdom literature likely had an influence on Moses and the Torah and the Old Testament of the Bible, written a thousand years later, as well as Jesus and Christianity. By the time of the Roman Empire, there was truly an integrated global economy in goods and ideas connecting the entire Mediterranean world with India, sub-Saharan Africa, and even China. From the Roman Empire onward, it is likely that there was some mutual influence on thought and philosophy of these diverse cultures.

Seneca and Marcus Aurelius would likely have read the works of Aristotle and were also deeply influenced by the Stoic school of philosophy founded in Greece shortly after Aristotle's death. However, the Roman branch of Stoicism was deeply molded and modified by the traditional ideals, beliefs, and virtues of the Roman Republic and early Roman Empire. Although they lived at the same time and in the same empire, it is unlikely that Seneca would have any knowledge of the teachings of Jesus. It is also unlikely that Marcus Aurelius would ever have read the Bible, although he does make one unflattering reference to early Christians in his writing. Muhammad was well aware of Jesus and his teachings, and Jesus is mentioned many times in the Koran, but he was clearly much less influenced by and likely hostile to the pagan writers who preceded Christianity. Zhu Xi was profoundly influenced by the teachings of Confucius and to a lesser extent by Buddhism. All later sages, from Elizabeth onward, would have been at least somewhat aware of and influenced by the teachings of all the sages who came before them.

The words "God" and "the Gods" appear commonly in these

maxims. It is important for the reader to understand that the writers may have had very different concepts of the divine. Ptah-Hotep would have been referring to the ancient Egyptian polytheistic pantheon led by the Sun God, Ra. In several instances, Ptah-Hotep's original text mentions Osiris and Horus by name, but in translation I have simply used the word "God." When Aristotle speaks of God or the Gods, on one level he would doubtless have been referring to Zeus and the related Greek pantheon, including Hera, Athena, Poseidon, Apollo, and Hades. However, on an intellectual level he would have been speaking of "the unmoved mover," a deist concept of a God who set the universe in motion but who does not meddle in human affairs. Seneca and Marcus Aurelius were Stoics, as were many of the Roman Senate and ruling class. At one level, these Stoics were likely speaking of the traditional Roman-Greek pantheon led by Zeus or Jupiter Optimus Maximus. However, Stoic philosophy also envisioned a less personal God that has more in common with deist or pantheist concepts. Pantheism is the belief that God is a part of everything and everything is part of God. Thus nature, the Earth, and the universe are God, and we each carry within us a spark of the divine. Confucius and Buddha were less concerned about theology and theological concepts of God, although they were very concerned about the divine world and man's place in it. However, they lived and taught in the polytheistic cultures of early China and India. Confucius often speaks of Tian, commonly translated as "heaven." The concept of Tian as used by Confucius may best be thought of as fate or the proper nature and ordering of the universe, which is itself worthy of respect and worship. Zhu Xi's religious beliefs were largely based on traditional Confucianist understanding but were also strongly influenced by Buddhism and by the ancient Chinese religion of Daoism that was founded by Lao Tzu in the sixth century BCE. Dao or the Way is focused on living in harmony with the underlying principles of the universe and embraces the important concepts of yin and yang.

In many respects, Jesus and Muhammad represent a sharp break with these earlier men. As a Jewish teacher, Jesus would have been thinking of Yahweh when he referred to God—the personal monotheistic God of the Jewish people. This is the traditional view of God that was modified and transmitted to Western civilization by Saint Paul and other early Christian writers. However, as the Christian religion gained acceptance within the late pagan Roman Empire, it also adopted many of the intellectual and spiritual traditions from the earlier polytheistic and Stoic society. Muhammad would have been thinking of Allah alone and strongly rejected the possibility of any other deities, multiple manifestations of a single divine force, or of the Christian Trinity.

Elizabeth was a devout but tolerant Protestant Christian who was deeply influenced by the teachings of Jesus. Franklin, Catherine, Washington, Goethe, Roosevelt, and Churchill would also have been strongly influenced by Christian theology and teachings, but also by the Enlightenment, the Scientific Revolution, and the newfound appreciation of the ancient pre-Christian pagan authors such as Aristotle, Seneca, and Marcus Aurelius. They were also all free thinkers who were devoted to independent thought and freedom of conscience. All of these later sages were likely closer to "a sect by myself,"[8] as Thomas Jefferson described himself—someone who felt comfortable developing independent religious beliefs, consistent with their unique personalities, instead of blindly following a received doctrine. Though raised as a Puritan Christian, Benjamin Franklin expressed views compatible with and supportive of polytheism, deism, and pantheism at different points in his life. Catherine readily converted from the Protestantism of her parents to Russian Orthodoxy with few misgivings. Washington was described as a modern Roman Stoic by some of his close contemporaries and refused to take Christian communion

---

8   *Thomas Jefferson to Ezra Stiles Ely.* June 25, 1819. Manuscript/Mixed Materials. www.loc.gov/item/mtjbib023541/.

throughout his life. Goethe and Churchill were profoundly influenced by Christian ethics but were also not particularly religious in a traditional sense. Roosevelt was a practicing member of the Protestant Dutch Reformed Church but was also a strong proponent of "Muscular Christianity."

Carver was a devout Christian with a deep faith in the divinity of Jesus. He firmly believed in the power of Christianity to bridge the gap between the white and black races. He also had a mystical reverence for nature and believed that the study of nature was also a study of God.

Gandhi was a devout Hindu and was deeply influenced by the Bhagavad Gita, a two thousand-year-old sacred text of that religion. In this deeply influential work, the Hindu God Krishna instructs the reader on the nature of the universe, the meaning of life, and how to live. Gandhi studied this book throughout his life, but he was also widely read and drew inspiration from many other religious and cultural traditions.

In short, I would urge the reader of these maxims to focus less on the theological questions of what each person means by God or the Gods, and more on the importance of having respect for what is divine and sacred in the universe, on the Earth, and in life. For, as the Buddha said, "What do I not teach? Whatever is fascinating to discuss, divides people against each other, but has no bearing on putting an end to suffering."[9]

---

9   Eknath Easwaran, *The Dhammapada* (Canada: Nilgiri Press, 2010).

LIVES

These biographies have been kept intentionally short and are only intended to highlight each person's major achievements and broadly illustrate their special character. The reader is encouraged to seek out a more comprehensive biography should they wish to learn more about any of these individuals. All eighteen sages led extremely full and influential lives, and their talents and accomplishments may make some of them seem almost superhuman. However, their lives should inspire even those of us with more average gifts to strive, to live to our full potential, and to leave a positive mark on the world. For as Gandhi said, "The difference between what we do and what we are capable of doing would suffice to solve most of the world's problems."[10]

Several of these people were founders of major world religions and some have even been deified. This was a common practice in the ancient world as a tribute to the accomplishments of great men and women or as an explanation of their greatness. Julius Caesar, for instance, was thought by the Romans to have become a God and to have ascended to heaven upon his death. His nephew and adopted son, the great Augustus Caesar, was hailed throughout his long reign as both the Son of God and the Prince of Peace for ending the Roman civil wars and founding the empire. Within a few generations, Jesus's followers adopted these same names to honor him. This tradition continues into recent times. Look only at the painting "The Apotheosis (Ascent to Godhood) of Washington" on the ceiling of the United States Capitol to see its more modern expression.

We know much more about the lives of the more recent sages than those from the ancient world. By necessity, the biographies of the earlier persons will not possess the same richness of detail. These short profiles are written as histories, under the same rules, expectations, and burden of proof required for researching any historical event.

---

10   Mahatma Gandhi, *The Little Black Book* (California: Renegade Publishing, 2015).

They are not intended as a religious biography or hagiography. As such, followers of Buddha, Jesus, and Muhammad will notice that many of the miracles and supernatural events attributed to them by their followers are not included. Also, where the weight of historical texts, historical context, or archeological evidence contradicts popular tradition or theological constructs, the biographies are true to the historic evidence. Fortunately, the noble character of these men and women is still clearly evident even after the accretions of myth, theology, and folklore are stripped away.

Ptah-Hotep

P tah-Hotep of Ancient Egypt is thought to have lived around 2400 BCE or roughly 4,400 years ago. Many scholars credit the writings of Ptah-Hotep as the oldest complete book on Earth that has survived to the present day. His writings are also the earliest complete example of traditional wisdom literature, which offers advice on how to live a successful life. This was a popular literary form for thousands of years in ancient Egypt. His maxims focusing on the virtues of moderation, kindness, fairness, honesty, generosity, and leadership may have influenced the later writers of the Bible's Old Testament.

We only know of Ptah-Hotep through the text attributed to him. However, a tomb has also been found bearing his name that dates from the late Old Kingdom. This tomb may be the author's final resting place. Ptah-Hotep was a chief minister to the pharaoh Djedkare Isesi, who ruled Egypt for over thirty years. Later Egyptians held Isesi in high regard for his significant administrative and religious reforms, as well as his successful early expeditions to the surrounding lands of Sinai, Nubia, and Punt.

Egyptian civilization was already centuries old by this time, and the first pyramids had already been built. It would stretch on for several thousand years longer before outside conquest and religious conversion, first to Christianity and later to Islam, extinguished the last vestiges of ancient Egyptian culture. Recent genetic testing performed on mummies shows the Egyptians of Ptah-Hotep's time were most closely related to other peoples living on the northeastern Mediterranean coast and Asia Minor (modern-day Turkey). He was undoubtedly a member of the scribal class and would likely have risen to the position of chief minister through ability rather than birth alone. The text states that he received many honors and favors from the pharaoh for his loyal service. According to the *Instructions*, Ptah-Hotep wrote down his maxims in old age for the education of his son. After a brief prologue describing his life, the text presents thirty-seven maxims that detail the values of the Egyptian upper class of his time.

Given the language and references in the text, some scholars believe it was written down several hundred years after his death. *The Maxims of Ptah-Hotep* has been transmitted to us on several ancient papyrus scrolls and one wooden tablet that were preserved by the extremely dry climate of Egypt. The earliest copy of the work is from the Middle Kingdom of Egypt (roughly 1800 BCE). Other copies exist from the New Kingdom from roughly 1300 BCE. This implies that the maxims of Ptah-Hotep were popular in Egypt and repeatedly recopied for at least a thousand years. Ptah-Hotep's instructions and other wisdom literature continued to be very popular in Egypt when Moses was raised in the pharaoh's court, the Israelites were led out of bondage, and the Jewish Torah (Old Testament of the Bible) was being written down a millennium later. Many scholars have noted particularly close parallels between the book of Proverbs in the Old Testament and another work of Egyptian wisdom literature called *Wisdom of Amenemope*. When Proverbs 22:17 urges the reader to "Pay attention and turn your ear to the sayings of the wise," it may well be referring to Ptah-Hotep and the other Egyptian wisdom writers who followed him.

Confucius (Kong Qiu)

Confucius is the Western name given to the Chinese philosopher Kong Qiu or Master Kong. Confucius was born around 551 BCE in the ancient State of Lu in modern northeast China. He is China's most famous philosopher and founded a school of thought and practice that has molded Chinese and broader East Asian culture to the present day. Confucian ideals stressing morality, compassion, etiquette, and social obligation formed the core curriculum of Chinese education, and Confucian knowledge was a requirement for government service in China for two thousand years, only ending with the overthrow of the last emperor in 1911. After being suppressed for decades under Mao Zedong and the Communists, Confucian ideals are again experiencing a revival.

Like Jesus and the Buddha, we have no writings from Confucius directly. The most trustworthy source of information about Confucius's life and teachings comes from a book called *The Analects*. This is a short collection of quotes, stories, and recollections written down by his disciples many years after his death. It appears to be a compilation of many authors and is not organized chronologically or by theme. It contains little biographical information but does offer a clear picture of Confucius's personality and teachings. The descriptions of Confucius in *The Analects* portray a dignified but humble man who was kind but very serious and strict about his teachings. He was a man who had a good sense of humor and frequently joked with his students. Confucius also loved music and would often sing and play instruments. He was fascinated by questions of how to live properly in this world but had little patience for speculation about theology.

Other early works about Confucius were likely lost during the brief despotic Qin dynasty, which tried to suppress Confucian ideals about the limits and moral obligations of government. Around the year 215 BCE, all Confucian texts were ordered burned, and over a thousand Confucian scholars were tortured and executed. The first official biography of Confucius existing today was written during the following Han dynasty, when Confucianism was adopted as the official state philosophy of China. However, this was about four hundred years after his death and so must be used with caution when attempting to reconstruct his life. Later writings about Confucius became ever more laudatory, and eventually he attained an almost god-like status in ancient China, with temples built and sacrifices conducted in his name.

Confucius's father died when he was a baby, and his mother raised him in poverty. He probably had to work as a manual laborer when he was young because *The Analects* state that he was skilled in numerous menial tasks. However, as a member of the lesser nobility, although poor, he was entitled to an education. He was likely trained in the Six Arts of ancient China: ritual, music, archery, charioteering, calligraphy, and mathematics. He was evidently an avid pupil. In *The Analects*, he states, "At fifteen I set my heart on learning."[11] Confucius married young and had several children. There is some indication in the early literature that he separated from his wife, but at least one of his children eventually became a devoted disciple.

As a young man, Confucius was already recognized for his skills as a teacher and had many students. He would not turn away anyone

---

11   Confucius, *The Analects,* translated by D. C. Lau (London: Penguin Classics, 1979).

who wanted to learn, including peasants, but he refused to teach those who would not make an effort, including nobles. Confucius taught how to be a virtuous man and how to govern with wisdom and justice for the good of the people.

Confucius lived during a period of upheaval and civil war, when traditional society and politics were in turmoil. At this time, the central government was weak, and more than ten small kingdoms perpetually fought for power. Chinese culture was already over a thousand years old in Confucius's day, and he hoped to restore Chinese society and government to the virtues of an earlier Golden Age of stability and peace. For him, the greatest role models all existed in the past. He likely thought of himself merely as a teacher of ancient wisdom; however, in reality he was an innovative thinker who developed a new philosophic tradition.

At the age of about fifty, Confucius finally was given senior positions in the government of his home country of Lu. He held posts as deputy of public works followed by minister of justice. He appears to have performed competently in both positions and had some successes, such as negotiating the return of lands to Lu, which had been taken by a rival kingdom. Although generally a proponent of leading by example rather than by force, as a minister, Confucius did have a few people executed for seemingly minor crimes by modern standards. Later Confucian scholars went to great pains to explain this seeming incongruity. He only worked for four or five years before falling out with the Duke of Lu, ultimately resigning in protest. It may have been that Confucius's unbending moral principles were not appreciated at the highest levels of the court.

Confucius left Lu and spent fourteen years in voluntary exile, traveling from kingdom to kingdom and offering guidance to government ministers and princes. He constantly searched for a ruler who would let him put his ideals into practice. He was ultimately frustrated in this dream and never again held high office. These were troubled times, and there was great adventure and significant risk in this wandering. Confucius often had to sleep in the countryside, sometimes went hungry, and was occasionally threatened with robbery and death. Confucius was always accompanied by a group of devoted disciples who sometimes found his simple lifestyle and teachings hard to live up to. As one said, "A good man must be strong and resolute, for his burden is heavy and his road is long, he takes benevolence as his burden, is that not heavy? Only with death does the road come to an end. Is that not long?"[12]

About twenty different disciples are mentioned in *The Analects*, but later tradition put this number at greater than seventy. Many went on to hold important posts in the government and others founded their own schools after Confucius's death. Confucius was eventually invited to return to Lu, perhaps through the influence of several of his former pupils who had achieved high government office. He continued to act as a court advisor and teacher until his death in 479 BCE at the age of roughly seventy. He may have thought himself a failure at death because he had not achieved the political and social transformation he had hoped for in China. However, much like Jesus and the Buddha, his disciples carried on his work and ultimately were successful in transmitting his message to the world.

---

12 Confucius, *The Analects*.

Buddha (Siddhartha Gautama)

Siddhartha Gautama was born around 500 BCE in a small kingdom at the foot of the Himalayan Mountains in modern-day Nepal. He later earned the title of the Buddha or "the awakened one" after he is said to have become enlightened to the true nature of the world. He is renowned as a teacher, great seeker of spiritual truth, and the founder of the Buddhist religion. The Buddha's teachings stressed acting with kindness and moderation, controlling our thoughts, and suppressing our desires in order to reach a higher state of happiness and contentment. His ideas were eventually transmitted to almost every country in Asia, even reaching distant Japan in the form of Zen. Buddhism has strongly influenced Asian religion and culture for thousands of years.

Although he taught a growing circle of followers for over forty years, we have no texts written directly by the Buddha. According to tradition, five hundred of his senior students gathered together shortly after his death to decide how to preserve and transmit his spoken teachings. This began a centuries-long tradition among the Sangha, the community of Buddhist monks and nuns, of memorizing and verbally transmitting his message. This oral tradition was finally written down several centuries later in a large body of works called the Pali Canon. This canon includes over five thousand of the Buddha's reputed lectures as well as discussions of Buddhist doctrine, rules, history, and philosophy. His life story can be pieced together with care using the Pali Canon and later written works from China. One of the most popular books in the canon has always been the Dhammapada, which means the path of truth or righteousness. This is a collection of the Buddha's sayings organized as a series of short and lyrical verses that show how to follow the trail blazed by Siddhartha Gautama. All of the quotes in this book are taken from the Dhammapada. For the Buddha, the spiritual and the virtuous life were closely intertwined and this is reflected in his teachings.

Gautama was a prince, born into wealth, power, and luxury; he trained to be a warrior and leader. He grew to be a strong, handsome, and intelligent man with a beautiful young wife and healthy newborn son. Gautama's life seemed charmed and his future bright, but he felt that there must be something more to existence. He was particularly troubled by the suffering he saw around him. He knew that sickness, old age, and death would eventually befall him and all those he loved. When he was twenty-nine, he decided to give up everything, abandon his family, and join the bands of homeless holy men who had forsaken all to try and find the truth. Like Jesus, he must have felt that family life was not compatible with his spiritual quest. Leaving the palace, he cut his hair, stripped off his fine clothes, and put on the simple garb of a peasant.

He began to study meditation with the masters of his time but quickly learned all he could from them. He then went into the wilderness, trying to reach enlightenment by taming his body through starvation, discomfort, and deprivation. After six long years, and near death, Gautama realized that he was no closer to his goal. In fact, both extreme deprivation and extreme pleasure were distractions that weakened and clouded the mind. Henceforth, he resolved to take the middle path and to live in moderation. His five followers, who had shared his hardships for several years, perceived this as a lack of will and left him in disgust.

No longer weakened and distracted by physical hardship, Gautama resolved to reflect and meditate until he truly understood the universe. He found a beautiful spot under a large tree overlooking a clear flowing river and vowed to remain there until he had attained enlightenment. Deep in meditation, he came not only to know but to truly believe what he called the four nobles truths: that life involves unavoidable suffering, that suffering is ultimately caused by desire and a refusal to accept the impermanence of all things, that humans can reach a state called Nirvana that is beyond the reach of suffering and desire, and that he had discovered the path to this state of ultimate happiness and contentment. It was at this moment his followers believe that Siddhartha Gautama had attained enlightenment and became the Buddha. Like the Confucian path for the good man, this was not an easy road to follow. It involved leading a strict moral life, feeling compassion for all beings, giving up all cravings, desires, and self-importance, and using rigorous meditation to control one's mind.

The Buddha initially felt that his achievement was beyond the reach of most people and hesitated to share his insights. However, eventually he came to believe it was his duty to teach what he had learned. He sought out his five former companions to share his insights with them. Like many others in the future, they were reportedly so impressed by the Buddha's peaceful, contented manner and logical explanations that they became the first members of the Sangha. This began a forty-five year teaching career and the conversions of thousands of monks and nuns to the new movement. The Buddha would teach to all who would honestly listen with no concern for wealth, caste, education, gender, or position. His father, foster mother, wife, and son all eventually became converts.

The Buddha was renowned for his ability to tailor his teachings to the unique experience and mind-set of his audience. There are several famous parables associated with the Buddha that, though perhaps mythologized, illustrate both his key messages and his methods. One student, Sona, strove for enlightenment with single-mindedness, to the detriment of all else. He was of noble birth and was renowned as a player of a stringed instrument called a vina. The Buddha brought him a vina with the strings set so loose that they made no sound and asked him to play. Sona humbly had to pass it back. The Buddha then took the instrument and tightened the strings so much that they could hardly be touched. Again Sona could not play. Finally the Buddha asked him to tune the instrument himself and play. Upon hearing the music, the Buddha exclaimed "Like the strings, you shouldn't let yourself be slack, but don't stretch yourself to the breaking point either. The middle way, lying between too much and too little, is the way of my path."[13]

On another occasion a poor mother came to the Buddha clutching a dead child in her arms and begging that he be brought back to life. The Buddha promised to help if the mother could bring him a mustard seed from a home that had never known death. Frantically searching from house to house, the women eventually realized that loss and grief are part of every person's life and she could not escape it. This realization put her on the path of the Dhamma and she became a follower. The one thing that the Buddha would not discuss was speculation about theology, metaphysics, and the nature of the Gods. He compared one particularly earnest pupil who kept asking such questions to a man shot by a poisoned arrow but who refused to have it pulled out until he knew the name, weight, and height of the shooter. As the Buddha said, his teachings were focused on pulling out the arrow of suffering—anything else was a distraction.

Well into old age the Buddha continued traveling about northern India and preaching in towns and villages. He lived a simple life, usually begging for his meals and sleeping in the open. Only in the rainy season, when it was too wet and muddy to travel, would the

---

13   Huston Smith and Phillip Novak, *Buddhism: A Concise Introduction* (New York: Harper Collins, 2003).

Buddha settle in one place. At the end of each rainy season he began walking once again, accompanied by a large group of monks. On one such journey in his eightieth year, he may have gotten food poisoning. Sensing death approaching, the Buddha lay down beneath a grove of trees and waited for the end to come. He asked his surrounding disciples if there was anything about his teachings they did not understand. As they mourned, he spoke his last words, "All things pass away. Strive for your liberation,"[14] and entered into a final meditation.

Buddhism remained one of many small sects in India until it was formally adopted as a state religion by the Emperor Ashoka, roughly two hundred years after the Buddha's death. According to tradition, the emperor was so appalled at the carnage he had caused in his wars of conquest that he renounced violence and took up the Buddhist cause. The Buddha's teachings began to spread across Asia, and eventually some followers even came to think of him as a god-like being. Perhaps the Buddha's legacy can best be summarized by one modern-day Buddhist leader, the 14th Dalai Lama of Tibet: "My true religion is kindness."[15]

---

14   Karen Armstrong, *Buddha* (New York: Penguin Books, 2001).
15   *Kindness, Clarity, and Insight: The Fourteenth Dalai Lama, His Holiness Tenzin Gyatso*, translated and edited by Jeffrey Hopkins and co-edited by Elizabeth Napper (Ithaca, New York: Snow Lion Publications, 2006).

Aristotle

Aristotle was born in 384 BCE in northern Greece. He is generally credited as the world's first true scientist and father of the scientific method. He tried to understand the world through observation and study rather than reliance on folktales, unseen spirits, or baseless hypothesizing. Aristotle was the founder of logic, helping establish a formal and reliable way to arrive at the truth. In his long career, he also studied and wrote on philosophy, political theory, the arts, and ethics. His influence on the Western and Islamic worlds was so profound that during the Middle Ages and Renaissance he was simply called "The Philosopher" or the "Master of Those Who Know." His political theories on the inherent virtues and vices of different forms of government deeply influenced the founding generation of the United States and helped inform the Constitution with its division of powers.

From ancient sources, we know that Aristotle wrote almost two hundred works on all of these topics. However, less than a third of his writings have survived, and much of what is available today appears to be compilations of notes from his lectures. Many of his most popular and influential books in antiquity did not survive the fall of the Roman Empire, and we only know of these works from quotes and favorable references made to them by other ancient authors. Most of the quotes in this book are translated from the *Nicomachean Ethics*, which was either written for or compiled by his son, Nichomachus.

Aristotle's father was the personal doctor to Alexander the Great's grandfather. He likely learned some anatomy and medicine from his dad. He spent part of his childhood at the Macedonian court and so would also have known Alexander's father, Phillip of Macedon, as a child.

At the age of eighteen, Aristotle was sent to Athens to complete his studies. This was just over a century after the Athenians and Spartans had defeated the Persians at the battles of Marathon, Salamis, and Plataea, ensuring the freedom of Greece and Europe. By this time, Athens had lost much of its political power in subsequent wars with Sparta, but it was still the center of learning for the entire Greek world. A generation before, Socrates had wandered the streets of Athens, challenging people to think for themselves and question the basis of their beliefs; in the process, he helped found Western philosophy (Greek for "love of wisdom"). Socrates's student Plato continued this tradition and established a permanent school in Athens called the Academy. Aristotle joined the Academy and was quickly recognized as a brilliant and original thinker. He spent the next twenty years studying and working under Plato's direction. However, he did not follow his teacher blindly. Unlike Plato, Aristotle was not satisfied with metaphysics, theology, and theorizing alone. He gained his inspiration by direct observation of the real world, followed by careful analysis and classification based on the similarities and differences between things.

With the death of Plato, Aristotle left Athens and spent a decade wandering the Greek world. He stayed several years on the island of Lesbos, eagerly studying and classifying its plants and animals. In Asia Minor he briefly established a school modelled after the Academy. Here he also married his first wife, Pythias, and they had a daughter together. Unfortunately, Pythias died while still young, but they were likely very close (Aristotle's will, written many years later, as his own death approached, directs that their bones be buried together). In roughly 342 BCE, he was invited back to Macedonia by King Phillip and asked to teach his thirteen-year-old son, Alexander. Aristotle was his tutor for three years. Alexander was by all accounts a genius but was also very self-assured, wild, and headstrong, so it is unclear what mark Aristotle left on the teen. However, there was undeniably a strong bond between them; throughout his conquests of the known world, Alexander the Great always remembered to send new animals, plants, and other scientific curiosities back to his old teacher.

Aristotle was now ready to return to Athens, but he did not want to rejoin the Academy. Instead he set up a new center of learning called the Lyceum, perhaps aided by money provided by Alexander. He gathered around him a group of like-minded philosophers and students, established one of the world's first great libraries, and maintained a zoo and a natural history museum. He liked to teach while walking around the covered walkways at the school, undoubtedly followed by a group of students straining to hear. The Lyceum also became a great center of scientific research directed by Aristotle. Almost all the major fields of science were explored and in many cases invented, including physics, geology, meteorology, botany, chemistry—but above all zoology. Roughly five hundred animal species were identified, described, and classified. As Aristotle said, "Every part of nature has its marvels."[16] Many of his discoveries about animal behavior and anatomy would not be reconfirmed for over two thousand years. He was the first to describe the Earth's water cycle, to argue that the Earth is round, and to recognize the slow changes that may occur to the landscape through geologic time. He got many things wrong as well. In a deep irony, these mistakes persisted for centuries because his works were taken as the absolute and unchangeable truth, even when they were contradicted by Aristotle's own methods of direct observation.

Aristotle also focused his attention on people—in particular, what makes individuals, governments, and societies successful. He studied

---

16   Aristotle, *Parts of Animals*, translated by A.L. Peck (Cambridge, Massachusetts: Harvard University Press, 1937).

the constitutions of roughly 150 city-states and countries to understand what the best forms of government were. In the *Nicomachean Ethics*, Aristotle identifies the search for happiness as the root cause of everything we do. He then explores how we can live a flourishing life that is happy, meaningful, and successful. Aristotle's ethics are centered on the highest classical pagan virtues of justice, courage, temperance (self-control), and prudence. Prudence in the ancient world meant having the wisdom and foresight to choose the right response or action for each unique situation. Generally, this required picking the moderate course between two extremes; for example, neither being overly boastful or overly meek in a given situation, but instead exhibiting proper pride.

With the death of his first wife, Aristotle began a relationship with Herpyllis in Athens. It is unclear if they ever married, but they had a son together. At the age of sixty, Aristotle almost certainly could look with satisfaction on his accomplishments and on the life he had built in Athens. However, his situation there was tenuous. He was not a citizen and, therefore, was not allowed to own land or vote. Athens was also tiring of the indirect rule of Macedonia. With the death of Alexander in Babylon, anger burst forth against Macedonia and anyone associated with the royal family. Aristotle was charged with disrespect for the Gods, the same charge that had been laid against Socrates some eighty years before. Socrates had refused to leave his native city. He was imprisoned and eventually forced to drink hemlock poison, dying in quiet and calm conversation with his friends. Aristotle did not intend to let the Athenians "sin twice against philosophy."[17] He fled to a Greek island with Herpyllis and his two children and died there a year later. His last will has survived and shows a man deeply concerned to provide for his living family and friends and to honor those who had died before him. Like George Washington

---

17 Joshua J. Mark, "Aristotle," Ancient History Encyclopedia, May 22, 2019, www. ancient.eu/aristotle/.

two thousand years later, he also directed that his slaves be freed and properly cared for.

Athens remained a center of learning for eight hundred years after Aristotle's death. In various forms, the schools founded by Plato and Aristotle continued and were attended by Roman aristocrats after that empire conquered Greece. However, their influence and vitality waned as a result of war, barbarian invasions, and the rise of Christianity. Their end finally came in 529 of the Common Era (CE) when Justinian, the Christian Emperor of Byzantium, attempted to eradicate the last vestiges of pagan belief and culture by banning the teaching of philosophy in Athens. Fortunately, the works of Aristotle survived to be broadly rediscovered in the Middle Ages, where they helped to spark the Renaissance in Europe.

Lucius Annaeus Seneca

Lucius Annaeus Seneca was born about 4 BCE in the Roman colony of Cordova in modern-day Spain. He is most famous as a philosopher, but he was also an accomplished statesmen and playwright. A large number of his writings on moral philosophy have survived, including texts on mercy, anger, tranquility, the happy life, providence, and the shortness of life. Seneca was also a prolific letter writer, commonly offering life advice to his friends, and over 120 of these letters have survived. Nine of his plays are also still in existence, and they had a particularly strong influence on Elizabethan play-wrights such as William Shakespeare. Seneca was a contemporary of Jesus, and his brother Gallio is mentioned in the New Testament of the Bible as having met the Apostle Paul. He is unlikely to have been very familiar with the early Christians and never mentions the new religion in any of his writings. However, one reason so many of his works have survived is because the early Christian Church approved of his moral teachings, and his manuscripts were carefully recopied in monasteries across western Europe throughout the Dark and Middle Ages after the fall of the Roman Empire.

Seneca was brought to Rome as a baby by his aunt and spent most of his childhood there. Along with his two brothers, he received a classical education to prepare him for work in government or the law. However, he most excelled at philosophy and became a lifelong convert to, and Rome's most eloquent advocate of, Stoicism. Unfortunately, his studies were interrupted by frequent bouts of asthma, and he spent several years in the Roman Province of Egypt in an attempt to regain his health. Upon returning to Rome as an adult, he finally began his career in government, serving in several mid-level posts, joining the Senate and gaining a reputation as a powerful public speaker. The empire at this time was dangerous for anyone with Seneca's fame, power, and ability. For the next thirty-five years, his life was in frequent danger due to court intrigues and the caprice of a series of despotic emperors. After one particularly acclaimed performance in the law courts, the mad Emperor Caligula became jealous and intended to have Seneca executed. Seneca only escaped because Caligula was persuaded that he would soon die anyway because of ill health. Seneca also angered the next emperor, Claudius. Upon gaining power, he banished Seneca from Rome on the almost certainly fabricated charge of adultery with Caligula's sister. The next eight years were bitter for Seneca. He lost his wife and a son while in exile, his career was in ruins, and he could be sentenced to death at any moment by Claudius.

Due to new maneuverings in the imperial court, Seneca was finally invited to return home in 49 CE, to take up duties as the official tutor of a young prince (and future emperor) named Nero. Little did he know that Nero would ultimately be responsible for his death fifteen years later. Things started well enough, and when Nero became emperor at the age of seventeen, he largely followed the advice of his old teacher. Nero was uninterested in working and left the task of governing the empire to Seneca and his friend Burrus, who was commander of the Praetorian Guard. Seneca introduced significant reforms into the Roman administration, and the provinces were well governed and the empire's frontiers secured. This first five years of Nero's reign were remembered in Roman history as a period of nearly unequalled good governance and prosperity. At this time, Seneca also wrote one of his most famous works titled "On Clemency" to the young emperor in an attempt to teach him to be merciful and just. Unfortunately, as Nero grew older, he gradually turned against his advisors, and his rule became ever more erratic, corrupt, and brutal. With the loss of influence, Seneca's position became precarious. He became the subject of new court intrigues, and rumors swirled about the enormous fortune he had amassed during his career. With the death of Burrus, Seneca's power was spent; he attempted to withdraw from public life, asking the emperor to let him retire and offering to give away his fortune.

He spent the last three years of his life traveling in southern Italy with his second wife, Paulina, writing, practicing philosophy, and trying to avoid Nero's attention. Seneca wrote several of his best works during this period. Ultimately, however, Seneca could not escape Nero's paranoid and vengeful behavior. After an attempted palace coup in 65 CE, Nero began a purge of all potential rivals and eventually demanded that Seneca also commit suicide. This was a common method of punishment in Imperial Rome and was considered much more honorable than being executed. On hearing of his death sentence, Seneca tried to calm his friends and family gathered around him saying, "Who was unaware of Nero's cruelty — after the murders of his mother and brother, it is only natural he should add the death of the man who raised and taught him."[18] He approached death calmly and counseled his wife to restrain her grief and not mourn for overly long. Regardless, she resolved to take her own life by the side of her husband but was physically restrained from doing so on Nero's orders. Seneca's death was not easy. He first cut open his veins, then took hemlock poison, and finally had himself immersed in scalding hot water to aid the loss of blood. His last act, like Socrates, was to pour some of the water out on the floor as an offering to the God Jupiter.

18   Publius Cornelius Tacitus, *The Annals*, translated by Moses Hadas (New York: Norton and Company, 1958).

Seneca has left the world many beautiful maxims and arguments calling for us to lead a virtuous, purposeful, and simple life. His words have inspired many through the ages to better themselves. However, he has also been charged with hypocrisy for his wealthy and extravagant lifestyle. He would have been the first to acknowledge that he was on the path to wisdom but had not yet fully arrived. However, he did try to lead a moral life amid immoral and dangerous times. Perhaps his greatest failing was embodied in the person of Nero, who despite Seneca's long efforts became a hated tyrant. Still, as Confucius said, "Rotten wood cannot be carved."[19] Not everyone could be as fortunate in his choice of pupils as Aristotle was with his student Alexander the Great.

---

19   Confucius, *The Analects,* translated by D. C. Lau (London: Penguin Classics, 1979)

Jesus of Nazareth

Jesus was born around 4 BCE in Roman Palestine in modern-day Israel. He was a carpenter and, later in life, a traveling Jewish rabbi and teacher. His teachings stressed kindness, modesty, piety, forgiveness and the value of good deeds in preparation for a coming judgment by God. He was also a religious reformer who felt that we should focus on how we treat others rather than on the strict observance of rituals, religious dogma, and tithing to religious organizations. He argued strongly against those focused on the external symbols of religious observance: "You have neglected the more important matters of the law—justice, mercy, and faithfulness" (Matthew 23:23). Although Jesus had only a small following at the time of his death, his disciples spread his moral philosophy and eventually established the Christian religion in his name.

Like Confucius and Buddha, Jesus did not write down anything directly. Almost all we know of his life and teachings is contained in the New Testament of the Bible. In the first hundred years after his death around 30 CE, there are only three brief references to Jesus or Christians in Imperial Roman records. The earliest written mention of Jesus outside of the Bible is by the historian Josephus, who wrote around 93 CE and who twice very briefly mentions Jesus in a much larger book titled *Antiquities of the Jews*. The next mention is in a letter from a Roman provincial governor (Pliny the Younger) to Emperor

Trajan in the year 112 CE. In this letter the governor asks the emperor for advice on how to prosecute Christians who are brought before his court. In 115 CE the famous Roman historian Tacitus wrote a history of Rome that also mentions Jesus. During the reign of Nero, large fires had destroyed much of the city of Rome and were reputed to have been set by command of the emperor. According to Tacitus, in order to divert attention from himself: "Nero blamed and inflicted severe tortures on a class of men hated for their abominations, who were called Christians by the [pagan] population. Christus, from who the name had its origin, was executed during the reign of Tiberius by order of the Procurator Pontius Pilatus."[20] This began centuries of persecution of this small community by the Roman government.

Much of the New Testament was written by, attributed to, or written about Saint Paul. Saint Paul's letters were created within a few decades of Jesus's death and so represent the earliest available written evidence about him. However, Paul likely never met Jesus before his death and says very little about the events of his life, so his writings are of limited use when trying to reconstruct a life history. For this reason, any history of Jesus's life must be based almost entirely on the Gospels of Matthew, Mark, Luke, and John. These books were written by Christians several decades after his death and were likely based on earlier oral traditions from people who had actually met Jesus.

The Gospels provide almost no information about Jesus's childhood but do indicate that he grew up and spent most of his life in Nazareth in the north of modern-day Israel. He was raised in this small village by his parents, Mary and Joseph, along with several brothers and sisters. He worked for most of his adult life as a carpenter, perhaps learning the trade from his father. Jesus does not appear to have ever married, but in later life he did have many devoted woman followers such as Mary Magdalene. When he was around thirty, Jesus

---

20 Publius Cornelius Tacitus, *The Annals*, translated by A. J. Church and W.J. Brodribb (New York: Modern Library, 1942).

was baptized by, and became a follower of, John the Baptist, a rabbi and preacher who spent much of his time wandering in the desert. After John was executed by the government, Jesus began preaching himself and spent several years in turn as a traveling rabbi and ethical teacher whose ministry was focused on his fellow Jews. He gained a reputation as a miracle worker. He was a powerful and charismatic speaker who generally taught in parables that could be easily understood by his audience. He was also kind and forgiving, and he would associate with the poor, outcasts, and people perceived as sinners. However, his success was not instantaneous or consistent. His own family did not appear to have initially accepted his teachings, and he was rejected in his home town of Nazareth. As Jesus himself said, "A prophet is not without honor except in his own town, among his relatives and in his own home" (Mark 6:4).

However, he persevered and eventually was joined by twelve devoted disciples, most of whom were fishermen from Lake Galilee or other working-class professions. Jesus was likely an apocalyptic preacher who may have believed that he lived in the end times before God was going to establish a new Jewish kingdom on Earth centered in Israel: "Truly I tell you, this generation will certainly not pass away until all these things have happened" (Matthew 24:34 and Mark 13:30). His teaching had great moral urgency because he felt his audience needed to reform their behavior as soon as possible to be ready for the imminent coming of the kingdom. This belief likely shaped his message of empathy and compassion embodied in his masterfully stated Golden Rule, "Do to others as you would have them do to you" (Matthew 7:12 and Luke 6:31). Unfortunately, it also meant that Jesus's teachings were not always focused on encouraging long-term success and stability for individuals, families, or communities. In the Gospels, he sometimes advises his followers to leave their families, to not have children, to give up all possessions, and to not worry about or plan for the future.

His preaching was largely restricted to rural areas and little towns in northern Palestine, and he was probably not well known outside of this small region. Jesus was also likely preaching in the Aramaic language and so was isolated linguistically from the broader intellectual and social discourse of the empire, which occurred in Greek and Latin. Toward the end of his life, he decided to join the annual pilgrimage to the provincial capital of Jerusalem for Passover. This was a time of intense political tension, as some Jews dreamed of being liberated from their oppressors and establishing an independent kingdom led by a Messiah, a great religious prophet, warrior or statesman who would vanquish the Romans. The Romans generally allowed internal self-rule for each of the provinces as long as they continued to pay their taxes, kept the peace, and allowed the empire to control foreign policy. However, each year the Roman governor would travel to Jerusalem for Passover with a large detachment of soldiers to maintain order and suppress riots or insurrections, which commonly broke out during the festival.

Jesus's revolutionary message and challenges to authority were disliked by many of the local religious and political leaders. He further angered the local authorities by causing a near riot at their most sacred temple and perhaps even worse by prophesizing that it would be destroyed in the near future (which turned out to be true). During the week before Passover, he preached at the temple and each day the size of the crowd who came to hear him grew. This likely provoked concern in the provincial government. On the night of Passover, Jesus shared the traditional feast with his disciples and then went to a garden to pray and meditate. There he was betrayed by one of his twelve disciples named Judas Iscariot and was seized in the garden while out of sight of the crowds. His loyal followers wanted to fight to protect him, but Jesus urged them to put away their weapons. After being taken into custody and briefly questioned by the local Jewish authorities, he was turned over to Pontius Pilate, the Roman

Governor of Judea from 26 to 36 CE, for trial. As described in all four Gospels, he was accused by the Roman provincial government of political treason and was sentenced to death for allegedly calling himself "The King of the Jews." If true, such a statement would have been seen as a direct challenge to the Roman administration and the authority of the emperor.

As was the empire's custom for convicted rebels who were not Roman citizens, Jesus was crucified and died on a wooden cross outside Jerusalem. Much like the death sentence of the sage Socrates handed down by the Athenian government about four hundred years before, Jesus was ultimately executed because of his provocative teachings and the threat they posed to the established order. This probably occurred around 30 CE when Jesus was only about thirty-five years old and had only been preaching for a few years. Like Confucius, he may have considered his quest to change his world a failure and a literal interpretation of some Gospel accounts would indicate that he died in despair (Matthew 27, Mark 15).

Given none of his teachings were written down at this time, his disciples were mostly poor and illiterate, and they were scattered and in hiding, this seemed to mark the end of his moral influence. However, several of his followers believed they saw or had visions of Jesus again after his burial and most even came to believe that he had been raised from the dead. It is difficult to draw any firm historical conclusions about exactly what happened because the four Gospels offer sometimes inconsistent descriptions about events after the crucifixion. There is also no mention of such an event by any pagan or Jewish writers of the time. However, it is clear that many of the original twelve disciples and new converts such as the Apostle Paul believed something profound had happened and continued his moral teachings, much like the disciples of Confucius and the Buddha. Many early Christians came to believe that this poor and modest teacher had been deified or was a demi-god like Hercules, and later Christians even came to believe that he was God. This small sect eventually became the Roman state religion under the Emperor Constantine three hundred years after Jesus's death. The core teachings of Jesus became the moral and spiritual basis of the Christian religion, which has inspired millions to pursue more virtuous lives and influenced history for almost two thousand years.

A literal interpretation of some early parts of the Christian Old Testament can appear to justify many wrongs including unprovoked military conquest, enslavement and genocide of other peoples (Numbers and Deuteronomy). However, these were written many centuries before Jesus's teachings, which moderated the sometimes-harsh commands of Moses and other early prophets. Although later history may provide examples of violence and bigotry perpetrated in the name of Christianity, this has occurred despite the words of Jesus not because of them.

Marcus Aurelius

Marcus Aurelius was born in 121 CE in Imperial Rome. At his birth the city was at the height of its power under the great Emperor Hadrian. Marcus would also become one of Rome's greatest emperors, known for his fairness, integrity, and devotion to duty. He was also a Stoic scholar and may represent history's closest approximation to Plato's ideal of a philosopher-king. However, his rule was not a happy one. He endured much personal tragedy in his family as well as plague, famine, rebellion, and war across the empire. During his twenty-year reign, there were only four years of peace along the frontiers. In many ways his life marks the beginning of the long decline and final collapse of Rome three hundred years later.

During these trying times, Marcus fortified his spirit through the study of philosophy. While living in rough military camps on the war-torn frontier with Germania, he wrote a short private manual for his own use called simply *To Myself* or *The Meditations*. This work, which miraculously survived, shows a profoundly conscientious man struggling to do good amid growing hardships. Although never intended for a broad audience, it has inspired many readers since it was rediscovered and first published during the Renaissance.

When his father died, young Marcus was raised by his grandfather, who was a prominent and wealthy Roman citizen. In his grandfather's household, he would have been exposed to many of Rome's ruling elite. When he was only six years old, something in his character had already caught the eye of Emperor Hadrian, who nicknamed the boy Verissimus or "Most True." Marcus was educated by the best tutors in Rome, who prepared him for high office. At the age of only sixteen, Marcus was adopted by the new emperor, Antoninus Pius, and by seventeen had gained the title of Caesar, along with a growing burden of responsibilities. At this time, it was the custom of each Roman emperor to choose his successor not from among his own children, but instead from among the most able and just of his subjects. This practice brought the empire to its zenith and led to almost one hundred years of unprecedented peace and prosperity for its citizens.

Antoninus gradually entrusted more and more power to Marcus until they were virtually co-emperors. Marcus also married Antoninus's daughter Faustina. However, it was not until Marcus's fortieth birthday that he became emperor in his own right. He showed himself to be an able, benevolent, and conscientious leader if not a great innovator. He promoted good governors and administrators at Rome and in the provinces. He made improvements to the Roman legal code, ensuring it was more just and increasing the protections for slaves, women, and children. He himself commonly sat as judge and was severe with grave offences but generally merciful for lesser ones. He disliked gladiatorial contests and reduced their number, extravagance, and even their deadliness by decreeing that only blunted weapons could be used. In sum, he ruled according to his vision of a country where "there is the same law for all, freedom of speech, and a kingdom that most of all respects the liberty of its people."[21] In his spare time, he continued to study philosophy and to focus on his wife and growing family of children.

---

21   Marcus Aurelius, *The Emperor's Handbook*, translated by C. Scot Hicks and David Hicks (New York: Scibner, 2002).

Unfortunately, after only a year in power, war broke out on the eastern frontier with Parthia (modern-day Iran). Marcus sent his adoptive brother along with several able generals to the Middle East to drive the Parthians back out of Roman territory. Victory was secured after five years of fighting, but the army returned from Asia with a terrible plague, perhaps the same Black Death that was to devastate Europe a thousand years later. It spread to all the provinces and may have killed up to one-third of the population. In the plague's wake came economic disruption and famine. The empire was also troubled by the continued growth of a new religious sect, the Christians, who would not make offerings to the emperor or the traditional Gods (a sign of loyalty and patriotism), and who often refused to join the legions and defend the frontiers. Marcus's reputation among many later historians was tarnished because of the persecution some Christians suffered under his government.

Perhaps sensing the weakened land to their south and facing destruction from other forces attacking them out of the east, the Germanic tribes in central Europe chose this moment to strike across the Danube River. They beat every army sent to stop them and eventually crossed the Alps into northern Italy. The very heart of the empire was threatened with conquest, and despite his dislike of violence, Marcus responded with decisiveness. To raise money, he auctioned off the imperial jewels. He enlisted all able-bodied men that could be found in Italy, including gladiators and even slaves, to fill the ranks of the plague-ravaged legions. He led the counterattack himself and eventually drove the invaders back across the Danube. Unfortunately, this was only the initial assault; more invasions followed.

Over the next decade, Marcus was only occasionally able to visit Rome, where he was honored as a beloved protector and hero by the people. During a brief visit to Athens, he was also able to fulfill what surely was a lifelong dream: he walked the streets of the ancient center of learning, attending lectures and discussing philosophy as a common student. On leaving, he endowed professorships for each of the great schools of wisdom: Platonic, Aristotelian, Stoic, and Epicurean. However, he was forced to spend most of his last years on the cold and violent northern frontier. During his time away from home, nine of his fourteen children died, and rumors circulated that his wife was unfaithful. His only surviving son, Commodus, was a violent, untrustworthy disappointment. Still Marcus persevered and, after many victories, was close to annexing several new provinces, extending the frontier and perhaps permanently removing the threat posed by the barbarian tribes to the north. However, on the verge of this great success, he fell ill and died near modern-day Vienna in 180 CE.

It was during this last decade of hardship and privation, while living in military camps along the Danube, that Marcus Aurelius wrote *Meditations*. The small book is a classic of Stoic philosophy. In it he exhorts himself to rise above life's challenges, to treat others with fairness, to be unafraid of death, and to lead an active life for the good of others. It is the survival of this very personal little book, rather than his deeds or leadership, that makes Marcus famous in our own day. In the end, Marcus's very compassion and humanity may have done the most to tarnish his legacy as a great statesman. Perhaps to avoid civil war, or the necessity of killing his only surviving son, Marcus allowed the worthless Commodus to become emperor upon his death. This broke the chain of good rulers who hand-picked their successors from the best and brightest of the next generation and thus helped usher in a century of chaos following his death.

Muhammad[22]

Muhammad was born around 570 CE in the town of Mecca in modern-day Saudi Arabia. He was the creator of the Koran and the founder of the Islamic religion. His teachings and moral example produced an ethical and spiritual renewal in Arabia. He was also the political founder of the Islamic Caliphate, which, shortly after his death, conquered the entire Middle East, Persia, and North Africa. The unification of this vast area enabled an economic and intellectual awakening that reached its peak three hundred years later. Baghdad became a global center of tolerance and learning where the science and wisdom of Egypt, Greece, Persia, and India was synthesized, preserved, and enhanced. Many Muslims believe Muhammad provides the supreme example of an ideal life.

Muhammad was born less than a century after the fall of the western Roman Empire to the barbarians. This was a violent, impoverished, and chaotic time, historically described as the "Dark Ages" in Europe and in Arabia as the "Days of Ignorance." At the time of his birth, the Arabs were fragmented into numerous tribes and clans that were constantly at war with each other. Arabia was also religiously divided with pagans, Christians, and Jews living uneasily together. Mecca and the Kaaba shrine were the center of the Arab pagan religion that worshipped Allah and numerous other Gods and Goddesses.

---

22   No image is provided for Muhammad in accordance with the Islamic prohibition of creating pictures or statues of prophets, which are believed to encourage idolatry.

Muhammad was orphaned as a very young boy and was raised by his extended family. His early poverty made him particularly sensitive to the plight of orphans and the poor. He prospered as a trader and merchant as his reputation for honesty and fair dealing grew. Muhammad eventually came to be called "The Trustworthy One" and was sought out to settle disputes between households, clans, and tribes. He married his first wife at the age of about twenty-five and seemed destined to become a wealthy businessman and the leader of his clan. He also liked to spend time alone in the desert in quiet contemplation. On one such retreat, at the age of forty, Muhammad had his first terrifying vision while in the wilderness. He feared he was crazy or possessed and rushed home to his wife. However, he eventually became convinced that one of Allah's angels was communicating with him. The angel urged him to become a prophet just like Moses, Noah, and Jesus, to reestablish the worship of Allah alone, and to lead an ethical revival amongst the Arabs. Over the next twenty years, Muhammad had many visions, which he would memorize and recite as Arabic poetry that was renowned for its great beauty.

Muhammad's first converts to the new religion were his wife and some members of his closest family. He had much less success converting the broader pagan, Jewish, and Christian communities around him. Like Jesus, he was evidently subjected to skepticism and ridicule in his hometown and gained a reputation as a mad poet, a charlatan, or a fool. However, he persevered and within a decade had successfully converted a core of avid believers. He had also caused the anger of many powerful people in Mecca, and in 622 CE had to flee for his life to the town of Medina, where he had been invited. Several hundred followers also emigrated with him. Here he became both a religious leader and eventually a ruler. He showed himself an able administrator and also began to raise an army to protect the city.

With his new responsibilities the tone and substance of the revelations recited by Muhammad also began to change. His visions became more focused on pressing legal, social, political, financial, and military matters. The fledgling Muslim community was urged to fight back (practice jihad) against those who oppressed or threatened them. This began almost a decade of bitter fighting between the unbelievers (infidels) and the Muslims. Muhammad proved himself to be a competent and sometimes ruthless military leader. However, in a practice unusual for his time, he often gave mercy to captured prisoners of war and showed clemency to those who submitted peacefully. He had several small military victories, but the Meccans still threatened to capture Medina and end Muhammad's religious revolution. Much of the Koran was first recited during these desperate times, when the fate of the small community still hung in the balance. In 630 CE the Muslims finally triumphed over their old enemies in Mecca and forced the conversion of the city. Muhammad made a last pilgrimage to the Kaaba shrine, purging it of any idols to Gods other than Allah, and reconsecrated it as the most holy site of Islam. All Muslims are still expected to make a pilgrimage to this shrine at least once in their lives if possible (the Hajj). In 632 CE Mohammed died, secure in the knowledge that he had defeated his enemies and firmly established his new faith throughout Arabia.

Shortly after his death, the first written version of the Koran was produced from a compilation of followers' memories of Muhammad's recitations. Each surah or chapter represents one of his revelations. The Koran and the Hadith (the direct quotes of Muhammad or remembrances of his actions) urge people to do good and to be truthful, honest, just, frugal, kind, and charitable. This moral guidance is most strongly focused on how Muslims should treat one another as members of the ummah (community of believers). As stated in surah 48, "Muhammad is the prophet of God and those who are with him are severe with infidels but compassionate among themselves."[23] Unfortunately, much of the book is also devoted to demonizing non-Muslims, be they pagan, Christian, or Jewish. There are over two hundred passages that describe how nonbelievers and those who do not obey God and his Messenger (Muhammad himself) are doomed to an eternity of humiliating torment in the scorching fire. Furthermore, anyone who does not share Muhammad's religious beliefs is repeatedly described in unforgiving terms such as evil, foul, unclean, treacherous, lying, crooked, foolish, hated by God, and without reason. More than ten times, the Koran exhorts the reader to avoid forming friendships or alliances with unbelievers. More than thirty times it urges the reader to actively fight nonbelievers with passages such as, "You who believe, fight the disbelievers near you and let them find you standing firm," and "If you do not go out and fight God will punish you severely" (surah 9).[24]

With the death of his first wife, Muhammad began to marry many converts, eventually taking about a dozen wives. According to historical accounts, he treated his wives with love, dignity, and respect; but the Koran also explicitly states that Muhammad and his followers are allowed to have sex with their female slaves (often unbelievers captured in battle), in addition to their wives (Surahs 23, 33, and 70). Unfortunately, this contributed to roughly a thousand years of Middle Eastern slave raids into Africa and Europe. Muhammad did try to improve the lot of the Muslim women of his time, condemning the custom of female infanticide and giving women limited legal rights in divorce and inheritance, where before they had none. He also exhorted men to be kind to their wives. However, taken out of context, these small but noble steps toward gender equality made fifteen hundred years ago can provide justification for the permanent second-class status of women today.

Regrettably, Muhammad insisted that the Koran, which he

23　*Al-Qur'an*, translated by Ahmed Ali (Princeton: Princeton University Press, 2001).

24　*The Qur'an*, translated by M.A.S. Abdel Haleem (Oxford University Press, 2004).

dictated, was directly transmitted to him from the one true God and that it is perfect. Furthermore, because he insisted that he was the last and greatest prophet, it can theoretically never be superseded, refined, or changed. Given this understanding, it is not surprising that some followers may take every word of the Koran as a literal command from God. This removes the book from the context of its reciter, a good man, trying to limit the worst excesses of his time and instead makes all statements in the Koran universally applicable to all times, places, people, and circumstances. Taken out of its historical context, the Koran can and has been used to justify violence and intolerance toward nonbelievers or other Muslims perceived as heretics. Certainly, most followers of Islam are tolerant of other cultures and beliefs, but they do so despite some of the words recited by Muhammad not because of them.

Zhu Xi

Zhu Xi was born in Fujian Province of southern China in the year 1130. He was the leading scholar and teacher of the neo-Confucian movement and synthesized faith, reason, and moral philosophy to revitalize Confucianism. His integration of metaphysical and spiritual elements from Daoism and Buddhism into Confucian thought re-established it as a dominant philosophy in China, Korea, Japan, and Vietnam for the next seven hundred years. His emphasis on careful observation of the natural world and objective reasoning to arrive at the truth also contributed to a scientific and industrial revolution during the Southern Song Dynasty a full five hundred years before the Enlightenment in Europe. Zhu is renowned as one of the "twelve wise ones" of Confucian tradition and is considered one of the most important thinkers in all of Asian history.

The Southern Song Dynasty (1127–1279) was a time of intellectual and economic ferment in China. Improvements in rice cultivation led to rapid population growth and the development of the world's largest cities. Industrial-scale steel and porcelain production, along with new inventions such as the compass, gunpowder, and advanced shipbuilding made China a commercial giant with a global reach. However, it was also a time of great insecurity. The northern half of China had been conquered by horse nomads from beyond the Great Wall, and the prosperous southern kingdom was under constant threat of invasion. The native Confucian and Daoist faiths had to compete with imported religions like Buddhism, Islam, and Christianity for converts. In response to these physical and cultural threats, Zhu and the broader neo-Confucian movement sought to strengthen traditional Chinese values and political independence.

Zhu was the son of a minor Song Dynasty official and was raised in the Confucian tradition by his parents. However, with the death of his father, the teenager was also instructed by Daoist and Buddhist scholars. He was a talented student; at the age of only nineteen, he passed the government's highest civil service exam, when the normal age for this achievement was thirty-five. He held several low- to mid-level government posts and had a reputation as an active and successful reformer. Zhu was also an outspoken critic of corruption and was in vocal disagreement with many imperial policies. In the end he was either not offered or refused more powerful positions. Instead, government patronage allowed him the time to pursue his passion as a scholar and teacher.

At the age of thirty, Zhu firmly rejected Buddhism and Daoism, which he felt focused too much on self-centered cultivation to the exclusion of broader moral responsibilities to the family, community, and country. Zhu wrote, edited, or annotated more than one hundred books. Most of these texts were philosophic and religious works, but he also dealt with history and the natural sciences. He sought, in part, to rescue the Confucian tradition from stifling bureaucratic control and refocus it on personal morality and spirituality. While acknowledging the critical importance of ethical norms and etiquette to organize and regulate society, he realized that these simple formulas do not work in all situations. For this reason, a good person must also be observant, thoughtful, and farsighted to choose the appropriate ethical response to each situation's unique circumstances. Zhu emphasized the impor-tance of studying history, culture, human behavior, and the natural world to understand the overarching patterns and principles governing the world. Only in this way, he felt, could one truly gain the wisdom needed to consistently make the right ethical choices.

Zhu's most important contribution to the renewal of Confucianism was almost certainly his selection of four books that he felt captured the essence of the philosophical tradition. These works were *The Analects*, *The Great Learning*, *The Doctrine of the Mean*, and *The Mencius*. Although these books were over a thousand years old, he felt that their ease, immediacy, and brevity would allow the essential teachings of Confucianism to reach the widest possible audience. He devoted much of his life to annotating these books, building a unified and consistent synopsis of their message. The Four Books and Zhu's commentaries became the effective Confucian canon in later centuries. He was still working to revise and refine his commentaries only days before his death in 1200.

His outspoken honesty had earned him many enemies in the imperial court, and he died in political disgrace. However, his reputation was fully restored within a decade, and his works rapidly regained their influence. The Four Books and Zhu's commentaries became required study for the imperial civil service exams and remained so until the twentieth century. His attempts to fortify Chinese society were severely tested shortly after his death when the Southern Song Kingdom was conquered by the Mongols, and all of China was subjected to almost a century of foreign rule. Ironically, despite Zhu's belief in careful observation and objective inquiry to arrive at the truth, his works eventually became an unchallengeable doctrine. This may have contributed to the stifling of further commercial, political, and scientific innovation in China and ultimately to the country's humiliation at the hands of other more dynamic powers like the United Kingdom and Japan in the nineteenth and twentieth centuries.

Elizabeth Tudor

Elizabeth Tudor was born in 1533 in Greenwich, England. She faced many dangers in her youth, but through caution and guile she survived to be crowned Queen Elizabeth I. For the next forty-four years, she and her councilors safely guided England through the bloody religious conflicts that ravaged the rest of Europe. England remained an island of relative stability and tolerance during her reign and emerged for the first time as a world power. Elizabeth supported exploration and the planting of the first English colonies in North America, which two hundred years later would give birth to the United States. Under her patronage and leadership, artists such as William Shakespeare flourished, forever enriching the English language. Her reign is rightly remembered as a Golden Age.

Elizabeth was known for her foresight and wisdom, but also for her wit, playfulness, and charm. She never married but had suitors from across Europe vying for her hand. She was hesitant to lose the power and independence she enjoyed as a single monarch; as she explained, "I will have here but one mistress and no master."[25] She eventually came to think of herself as being married to her country.

In an age when most women were expected to be quiet, subservient, and docile, Elizabeth loved to hunt, ride, and dance. She was an

---

25 Anne Somerset, *Elizabeth I* (New York: Anchor Books, 2003).

excellent musician, known for her skill on the lute and virginals (a type of harpsicord). She was also fluent in French, Italian, Latin, and (to a lesser extent) Greek and Spanish. The court was also renowned for its sophistication and amusements. Several of Shakespeare's most famous plays, including *A Midsummer Night's Dream* and *Twelfth Night*, were first performed in front of Elizabeth. She enjoyed jokes and banter, often spontaneously composing poetry or rhyming responses with nobles, courtiers, and ambassadors. Hundreds of Elizabeth's written letters, poems, and speeches have survived. Even many of her conversations were written down by participants. In these communications she offered much good advice and direction to her administrators, military leaders, ambassadors, friends, and fellow heads of state.

Elizabeth's mother was Anne Boleyn, the unfortunate second wife of King Henry VIII. Anne was executed on likely fabricated charges only two years after Elizabeth's birth so Henry could marry his new favorite. In his quest for a male heir, Henry also had Elizabeth declared illegitimate. In the ten years following Henry's death, his three children, each from a different wife, were used as pawns by various factions as they maneuvered for control of the throne. Like the rest of Europe, England was also torn by violent conflict between the Catholic Church and the new Protestant movement. Under the short-lived rule of Elizabeth's Catholic sister, Mary, many prominent Protestants were burned at the stake and Elizabeth's own life was frequently in jeopardy. After a failed coup attempt, the Protestant Elizabeth was imprisoned in the Tower of London, a place which many entered but few left alive. Her life hung in the balance, and it was only by hiding her true beliefs and carefully managing perceptions that she was able to save herself. However, her half-sister remained suspicious, and Elizabeth's life was in constant danger until Mary died in 1558.

At the age of twenty-five, Elizabeth was crowned queen and immediately began reforming the government. She had inherited a weak kingdom, divided by religion, near bankrupt, at war with France, and without allies. Fortunately, she was a shrewd judge of character and rapidly assembled a group of able and loyal advisors led by William Cecil who were to serve her for decades. She was very frugal and restored the country's finances. Elizabeth was also a religious moderate who disliked the extremes of the Protestant Puritans as much as those of the Catholic Counter-Reformation. As she described it, "There is only one Jesus Christ, and one faith, and all the rest is a dispute over trifles."[26]

A religious settlement in her first year as queen established a national church that, though Protestant, retained much of its original Catholic character. This moderate reform, along with Elizabeth's relative tolerance, allowed England to avoid the worst of the religious conflicts that were to rack western Europe for almost a century. A religious civil war in France during Elizabeth's reign may have killed ten percent of the population, while an estimated one-third of the population of Germany died in the bloody Thirty Years' War as rival Catholic and Protestant armies from Sweden, France, Spain, and Austria invaded and ravaged the countryside in an attempt to gain religious and political dominance.

Despite the queen's moderation, in 1570 the Pope not only excommunicated Elizabeth, "the servant of wickedness,"[27] but also released all Catholics from their allegiance to her government. This act encouraged many assassination and coup attempts. At the center of many of these plots was Elizabeth's Catholic cousin, Mary Queen of Scots. Elizabeth resisted the urging of her counselors to execute Mary for almost twenty years, but in the tense year of 1587, she finally realized that "If Elizabeth is to live Mary must die."[28]

---

26 Anne Somerset, *Elizabeth I*.

27 Anne Somerset, *Elizabeth I*.

28 Frederick Chamberlin, *The Sayings of Queen Elizabeth* (London: John Lane The Bodley Head Ltd., 1923).

Whenever possible, Elizabeth tried to avoid open conflict and instead relied on skillful diplomacy to serve her country's interests. Such was her reputation that the exasperated Pope Sixtus V exclaimed, "She is only a woman, only mistress of half an island, and yet she makes herself feared in Spain, by France, by the Empire, by all."[29] However, eventually even she felt compelled to directly support Protestant Holland in its war of independence against the might of Catholic Spain, the great military superpower of the age. She sent a small English army to help ensure Dutch independence. She also released her "Sea Dogs," wild adventurers and buccaneers led by Sir Francis Drake and John Hawkins, to open trade routes to the New World, raid Spain's ports, and prey on treasure ships sailing from the Caribbean to Europe.

The crisis reached its climax in 1588 with the sailing of the Spanish Armada, an invasion fleet of 130 massive warships with the intent to conquer England, install the Inquisition, and establish a vassal state. The Sea Dogs fought a running battle with the Armada in the English Channel and harassed the enemy fleet until it was scattered and finally destroyed by North Atlantic storms. On land Elizabeth waited with an army, hoping to repel the better equipped and trained Spanish invaders if the sea battle went badly. Much like Churchill 350 years later, she faced a "valiant, disciplined and ruthless"[30] foe. She also roused her country to war with stirring words: "I know I have the body of a weak, feeble woman; but I have the heart and stomach of a king—and of a king of England too, and think foul scorn that Parma or Spain, or any prince of Europe, should dare to invade the borders of my realm."[31]

---

29   Anne Somerset, *Elizabeth I*.

30   Richard Langworth, *Churchill by Himself: The Definitive Collection of Quotations* (New York: Public Affairs, 2008).

31   L.S. Marcus, J. Mueller, and M.B. Rose, *Elizabeth I, Collected Works* (Chicago: University of Chicago Press, 2000).

Elizabethan England also looked to new opportunities in the far west. In 1580, Francis Drake completed a voyage around the world and returned to England loaded with Spanish treasure. In 1584, Sir Walter Raleigh, a dashing explorer and adventurer, was granted the charter for the colonization of North America. Elizabeth also provided him with the financial resources to equip repeated voyages to the New World. Between 1584 and 1588, Raleigh sent at least eighteen ships across the Atlantic, at a time when this effort was almost comparable to a trip to the moon today. Raleigh's explorers mapped the entire coast of modern-day North Carolina and Virginia. Native Americans traveled back to London, where they created great excitement when they were received at Elizabeth's court. Some Indian tribes even swore loyalty to her, and Elizabeth acquired the proud title of Weroance, or grand chief, of the Virginia colony (named after the Virgin Queen). In 1587, a full-fledged colony was established on Roanoke Island on the Outer Banks of North Carolina. The colony's support ships set sail, promising to return within months with additional supplies. At this point disaster struck, for the threat of the Spanish Armada prevented any relief ships to be sent for three full years. When the first rescuers did arrive, they found an abandoned fort but no trace of the colonists. The mystery of the "lost colony" haunted Elizabethan England and remains unsolved to this day. Nevertheless, the knowledge and experience gained from these early settlement attempts contributed to the eventual success of the Jamestown Colony, founded just four years after Elizabeth's death, on a site recommended by Raleigh's explorers.

The last years of Elizabeth's reign were not happy ones, as the war with Spain dragged on, taxes had to be raised, and harvests failed. The queen found herself ever more constrained by financial and diplomatic worries. Elizabeth's caution, which had served her so well in the past, may have also prolonged the war with Spain and ultimately prevented England from gaining victory. With her death in 1603, the country welcomed King James I to the throne. However, it did not take long before Elizabeth was remembered with nostalgia and the reign of Good Queen Bess, the Virgin Queen, was recalled as a high point in English history.

Benjamin Franklin

Benjamin Franklin was born in 1706 in Boston, Massachusetts. He was a renowned scientist, inventor, author, publisher, and diplomat. His groundbreaking research into electricity and its relationship to lightning earned him the title of the Modern Prometheus and made him the most famous colonial American of his age. He was also instrumental in the success of the American Revolution and the founding of the United States. As the rebellious colonies' first ambassador to France, he almost single-handedly gained recognition, financial aid, and military support for the struggling independence movement. As the chief negotiator of the peace treaty with Britain, he secured through diplomacy the victory that George Washington had won on the battlefield.

Franklin was renowned as a self-made man who had started with nothing but accumulated fame and fortune through hard work, intellect, and thrift. Almost all of his images show a heavy-set, balding elderly man, but throughout most of his life Franklin was known for his strength, built up by daily manual labor and his (then unusual) hobby of swimming. In his youth, he had seemingly boundless energy and could work all day, study at night, and still find time for friends, family, and volunteer projects for his community.

Franklin was married to Deborah Read for over forty years, and they raised three children together. Unfortunately, their later marriage was probably not a happy one. They were separated for many years as Franklin served the colonies in London as an informal ambassador before the revolution. Deborah was too afraid of sea travel to make the often-harrowing crossing of the Atlantic, while Franklin repeatedly declined to return to Philadelphia. He did not come home until after her death. However, he remained close to his children and grandchildren, several of whom accompanied him on his extended missions to Europe.

He was a prolific writer and focused much of his energy on political, religious, and scientific topics. He was also fascinated by self-improvement and morality. Franklin felt democracy was a very fragile institution that could not survive unless every generation of its citizens were principled, for, "Only a virtuous people are capable of freedom."[32] He himself focused on thirteen key virtues that he tried to constantly improve upon but did not completely master: temperance, silence, order, resolution, frugality, industry, sincerity, justice, moderation, cleanliness, tranquility, chastity, and humility. The most famous expression of Franklin's moral thoughts are the maxims he wrote for his *Poor Richard's Almanack*. Franklin printed this popular annotated calendar for twenty-five years and produced hundreds of adages based upon his astute observations of human nature, virtues, and vices.

Franklin was born into a very large and very poor family. He was a gifted child, and his parents decided to devote some of their meager resources to his education. However, after only two years of formal schooling, economic hardship forced Franklin to quit. At ten years of age he began work in the family's candle-making business. When an older brother established a printing shop in Boston, Franklin's father

32   H.W. Brands, *The First American: The Life and Times of Benjamin Franklin* (New York: Anchor Books, 2002).

agreed to send young Benjamin to join the enterprise as an apprentice. He took immediately to the business and showed great talent in both the physical art of printing and the intellectual component of composition and writing. He also found time in the early morning and at night to continue his informal education by diligently reading any books he could find. Apprentices at this time had almost no freedom and few legal rights, and they were often treated little better than slaves during the terms of their contract. To make matters worse, his brother was a harsh and sometimes abusive master who was jealous of his younger brother's talents. At the age of seventeen, Benjamin decided to break the contract and flee Boston as a fugitive.

Perhaps in rejection of the rigid society of Puritan Boston, Franklin chose to settle in open and tolerant Quaker Philadelphia. He arrived tired, dirty, and hungry, with only the clothes on his back and a single Dutch dollar in his pocket. From this impoverished start he first found employment as an assistant printer. Through five years of hard work, diligent saving, and a careful cultivation of his reputation, Franklin was eventually able to raise the capital needed to found his own printing works, which quickly prospered. He steadily grew his business until, at the age of forty-two, Franklin was able to retire and pursue his passions in science, invention, and civics without distraction.

Franklin immersed himself into the study of electricity, developing the first primitive batteries and electric motors, and becoming the first to describe electrical phenomenon in terms of positive and negative charges. He hypothesized that lightning was also, in fact, an electrical phenomenon and correctly described the mechanism by which it was generated. He and his son then went about proving this idea with the famed experiment of flying a kite with a conducting string into a thunderstorm. Imagine their delight when the device succeeded in bringing an electrical charge to the large key tied at the base of the string. Franklin was not satisfied with theoretical science for its own sake and always looked for practical applications. The kite experiment led directly to his invention of the lightning rod, little changed today from his original design. He also invented a much more efficient wood-fired stove whose basic design, with improvement by later inventors, is still in use. This stove directly improved the health and comfort of colonial homes while reducing the insatiable demand for firewood that was contributing to the rapid deforestation of the colonies. His other notable inventions include bifocals and a novel musical instrument called the armonica. Music was created by rubbing wetted hands across a rotating keyboard of thirty-seven differently sized glasses, each of which produced sound at a different pitch. The instrument became a sensation and, much like Goethe's poetry, inspired composers such as Mozart and Beethoven to incorporate its haunting tones into their works.

During his life Franklin made the Atlantic crossing six times and became interested in using ocean currents to make voyages more rapid and safe. On these crossings, it was a common sight to see Franklin or one of his grandchildren regularly lowering instruments over the ship's side to measure ocean temperature. He and his collaborators became the first to produce a reliable map of the Gulf Stream. Franklin chose not to profit from any of his discoveries or inventions for as he stated, "… as we enjoy great advantages from the inventions of others, we should be glad of an opportunity to serve others by any invention of ours, and this we should do freely and generously."[33] Franklin also gave freely of his time as a community organizer, helping to establish some of the first fire-fighting companies, hospitals, libraries, and universities in the American colonies.

Franklin became increasingly interested in politics as he grew older. Though still very loyal to the British crown, he became an early proponent of political union for the thirteen colonies. In 1757, Pennsylvania sent him to London as their agent, where he effectively

---

33   H.W. Brands, *The First American: The Life and Times of Benjamin Franklin.*

acted as the colony's informal ambassador. In later years he was also asked to represent the interests of Massachusetts, New Jersey, and Georgia to Parliament and the king. For almost twenty years he stayed in London, developing close friendships and strong ties with the scientific, artistic, and political leaders of Great Britain.

As tensions grew between the colonies and the British government, Franklin increasingly found himself in the middle trying to bridge the widening gap. In his quest for reconciliation, he found himself distrusted by both sides, particularly by uncompromising colonial firebrands like Samuel Adams and the Sons of Liberty in Massachusetts. In 1774, shortly after the Boston Tea Party, Franklin was summoned to explain himself and the colony's rebellious behavior to the prime minister and the senior councilors of the British government. The hall was filled with the most powerful men and women in England, eagerly waiting to see America's most famous citizen publicly humiliated. Franklin appeared, prepared to make one last case for compromise, but instead he was insulted, vilified, and accused of treason for nearly an hour. He stood silently, showing no emotion as he was called a thief, liar, traitor, and outcast to the laughter and jeering of the audience. This searing experience convinced Franklin that cooperation was no longer possible and that the colonies must be free.

He sailed for home in 1775; only a year later, he helped to draft the Declaration of Independence with Thomas Jefferson. Now more than ever, the unity of the colonies was paramount, for as Franklin declared, "We must indeed all hang together or most assuredly we shall all hang separately."[34] By signing the declaration, Franklin was putting the lives of himself and his family at great risk. It also alienated his only surviving son, who was then the royal governor of New Jersey and stayed loyal to the British king. Although they were to meet again after the war's end, the rift between them was never healed.

---

34 Benjamin Franklin, *Quotations of Benjamin Franklin* (Bedford, Massachusetts: Applewood Books, 2003).

To help bind the new country together, the Continental Congress appointed Franklin as its first postmaster general. However, after only two years at home, he had to board ship once more—this time as the Americans' first ambassador to France. The Atlantic voyage almost killed the seventy-year-old Franklin, but on arriving in Paris he plunged into his diplomatic duties. Over the next five years he came to symbolize the American cause in the minds of the French people and government. He was celebrated as a rustic backwoods philosopher and became the toast of Paris. Franklin, along with the continued survival of George Washington's small army, convinced the French to discreetly supply arms and money to the struggling independence movement and later to provide open support with treaties, armies, and fleets. French aid was decisive for America's victory but almost bankrupted the government of King Louis XVI and ultimately contributed to the monarchy's downfall in the French Revolution. With the victory of Washington and Rochambeau at the Battle of Yorktown, the British were at last ready to negotiate. Franklin once more led the diplomatic effort. The negotiations went on for more than a year, but the aging Franklin applied all of his energy and wisdom to ensure a favorable outcome. Ultimately, all of the Americans' key conditions were met: full independence, withdrawal of British soldiers from American soil, and extension of the new country's borders all the way to the Mississippi River.

Franklin was at last ready to come home, landing in Philadelphia in 1785 and hoping to spend "the little remainder of my life with my family."[35] He arrived in North America in time to play a leading role at the Constitutional Convention. Like Washington, Franklin had also grown increasingly uncomfortable with the institution of slavery. Although he had owned several slaves as a young man, he had freed them during the revolution. After returning home from Europe, he

---

35   H.W. Brands, *The First American: The Life and Times of Benjamin Franklin*.

began to actively campaign against slavery and became president of Pennsylvania's abolitionist society. In 1790, Franklin's last public act was the submission of a petition to the newly established government calling for an immediate end to the Atlantic slave trade. His dream was eventually fulfilled in 1808 when the national government formally banned the importation of any new slaves into the country. He died a few months later at his home in Philadelphia with his grandchildren at his side.

Catherine the Great

Catherine was born in 1729 as Sophie Friederike Auguste von Anhalt-Zerbst in the city of Stettin on the modern-day German–Polish border. Although raised as a minor German princess, she entered the ruling family of the Russian Empire as the young wife of the future czar. Her marriage was deeply unhappy, but she fell in love with Russia and its people. After deposing her estranged husband, Catherine directly ruled the empire for thirty-four years. As empress, she worked tirelessly to improve the country's administrative, legal, education, and medical systems. She greatly expanded the empire's borders through wars with the Ottoman Empire in the south, annexation of Polish lands to the west, and settlement as far east as Alaska. Her government and military reforms helped turn Russia into a great world power for the first time in its history.

Although Catherine's family was not wealthy, they did provide her with a good education in the hopes of a marriage with some powerful nobleman. Her parents were doubtless overjoyed when Catherine was summoned to the Russian court in Saint Petersburg to be the wife of Crown Prince Peter. At this point in her life, the fourteen-year-old girl was little more than a pawn in the political intrigues of Prussia, Austria, Russia, and Sweden. The young Catherine must have felt frightened and powerless as she left her native country for an unknown distant land with a different religion, language, and customs to meet a future husband she did not know. However, her intelligence, ambition, and political skills became evident almost immediately. She devoted herself to learning the Russian language, converted freely to Russian Orthodoxy over the objections of her Protestant family, and began building friendships and alliances within the court. After her religious conversion at age sixteen, her name was changed to Ekaterina (Catherine) Alekseevna and she was married. Her husband was a neurotic, childish, and often cruel young man whose face was also horribly scarred by smallpox. Although their marriage lasted for seventeen years, it only brought Catherine sorrow, humiliation, and loneliness. She was a virtual prisoner in her small palace apartments, her friendships were restricted, and she was not even allowed to exchange private letters with her parents. At one point, unable to tolerate her miserable conditions any longer, she begged to be sent home to her family. She consoled herself with hours of horseback riding, hunting, and reading. She read any books she could acquire but especially loved the ancient classical authors as well as the writings of the new Enlightenment philosophers from western Europe.

With the death of the old Empress Elizabeth, Catherine's husband finally become the czar in 1761. Although he was the grandson of Czar Peter the Great, he had also been born and raised in a small German country. Unlike Catherine, he refused to learn Russian and openly proclaimed a dislike for his adopted country. Even worse, he idealized the King of Prussia, with whom the empire was at war. He was hated by much of the Russian army, church, and nobility. The first months of his reign were marked by erratic behavior and a disastrous foreign policy. He also publicly stated that he intended to divorce his wife and force her into a convent. Only six months into his rule, a revolt broke out in the military garrison of Saint Petersburg. Catherine rode with the rebellious soldiers to arrest her husband. The czar was forced to abdicate and later died under mysterious circumstances. Although it is unlikely that Catherine ordered the murder, her followers were responsible, and she was branded a regicide by much of Europe. Her position was extremely precarious. She was a foreigner with no Russian blood, and she had a tenuous legal claim to the throne. She hurriedly had herself coronated in Moscow and began to solidify her popularity with the Russian people, who eventually came to call her "Little Mother."

Peter may have been impotent, and the loveless marriage may not ever have been consummated. During their marriage, Catherine had come under increasing pressure to produce an heir to the throne. She was eventually encouraged to take a lover from among the Russian nobility. Over her long life she had more than ten public paramours and had three children from three different fathers, scandalizing all of Europe. Her actions were similar to many kings of her time, but because of her sex and her great successes in international affairs, she was held to a less forgiving standard. In many ways she faced the same dilemma as Queen Elizabeth I of England. If she were to officially marry, she would lose much or perhaps all of her power to her husband. Undoubtedly, the great love of her life was Grigory Potemkin. He was devoted to her, and they may have been secretly married. For most of her reign this brilliant, talented, and energetic man supported Catherine in many of her greatest endeavors.

Unlike many of her predecessors, Catherine took an active role in the government. She would rise before dawn and commonly work twelve hours per day. Her ministers were both amazed and perhaps concerned at the attention to detail, penetrating questions, and confident decisions of this woman with no prior government experience. She first needed to refill the state treasury and address the budget deficit. She eliminated trade monopolies that had been granted to wealthy families, voluntarily gave up her own personal allowance, and brought church lands, which covered almost one-third of the country, under direct government control. She then unleashed a torrent of reforms across Russian society, including the founding of an academy of sciences; establishment of a central bank; elimination of trade restrictions; reorganization of the provinces to improve government efficiency; and promulgation of a charter of towns to help promote urbanization, establish local self-government, and offset the power of the nobility. She established the first national education system that was open to all free, talented citizens. Catherine also founded a school for midwives and established the Smolny Institute, the first state-financed school for women's higher education in Europe. To improve Russian agriculture, she encouraged the immigration of central European peasants, who introduced modern farming practices into the country.

She also had agents scour Europe to bring talented scientists, doctors, engineers, and artists to enrich Russian commerce and culture. When Catherine learned that some doctors in Britain were experimenting with the inoculation of healthy people with the pus from someone who was sick with smallpox, she became determined to test the vaccine on herself and demonstrate its efficacy to the skeptical Russian people. In secret she brought a leading doctor from London and, to the horror of her closest advisors, had herself successfully treated. The practice became widespread across Russia within her lifetime, contributing to the eventual eradication of this deadly, highly infectious disease.

Early in her reign, Catherine called a national assembly to help rewrite the empire's antiquated legal code. In preparation, she wrote a set of detailed instructions for the delegates based upon Enlightenment principles of equality, liberty, and rationality. Unfortunately, the assembly ultimately proved a failure. Both Catherine and her government failed to meaningfully improve the lot of serfs in Russia. Serfs were native-born slaves who could be bought and sold along with the land to which they were tied. They had almost no legal protections and were often subjected to extreme brutality at the hands of their masters. They made up the majority of Russia's population, but Catherine did not feel she could so directly challenge the nobility whose wealth was built upon serf labor. Her neglect of just over half of Russia's citizens is one of the most substantive and persistent criticisms of Catherine's rule. It was not until 1861 that Catherine's great-grandson Czar Alexander II, nicknamed "the liberator," emancipated all of Russia's enslaved serfs.

In her limited free time, Catherine was also a prolific writer of memoirs, plays, and letters. She was fluent in German, Russian, and French and kept up an active correspondence across Europe with philosophers, rulers, administrators, and friends. Over six thousand of her letters have survived and offer unique insight and wisdom from one of the most influential women of all time. Among her most famous correspondents were the philosophers Voltaire, Grimm, and Diderot. They admired her but also sought to reinforce Enlightenment ideas on progressive governance. She was receptive in her early reign, but she could also become exasperated with their high ideals, which were often impractical in the real world, for, as she wrote, "You work only on paper, which accepts anything, is smooth and flexible and offers no obstacles either to your imagination or to your pen; while I, poor Empress, work on human skin, which is far more sensitive and touchy."[36]

Under Catherine, Russia had an active and often aggressive foreign policy. Her greatest successes were achieved against the Ottoman Empire to the south. The Ottomans twice declared war on Russia and were twice soundly defeated. Russia extended its territory to the north shore of the Black Sea and gained an exceptional deep-water port in the Crimea. The conquest of the Muslim Tatar Kingdom in Crimea also ended over three hundred years of slave raids that had likely sent more than a million eastern Europeans into Turkish and Middle Eastern slave markets. This "harvesting of the steppes" had

---

36 Henri Troyat, *Catherine the Great* (New York: Penguin Group, 1994).

depopulated and impoverished much of Poland, Ukraine, and southern Russia. Upon liberating this vast, empty land, Grigory Potemkin immediately began to create new prosperous and populous provinces for the empire. In just twenty years, over one hundred new towns were established; roads, shipyards, and schools were built; and a powerful Black Sea fleet was launched to shield the region from further Ottoman incursions. To the west, Catherine helped orchestrate three partitions of Poland. The first two annexations brought Eastern Orthodox populations into the empire, but the final partition seized lands with a Catholic Polish majority. To widespread international condemnation, Catherine, along with Prussia and Austria, had extinguished the ancient and proud Polish nation from the map of Europe. It was not to regain its independence until after World War I. However, she was praised in other areas of foreign policy. Her "Declaration of Maritime Neutrality" guaranteed freedom of the seas during the American Revolution and was quickly adopted by most of Europe. She kept Russia out of several large European wars and wisely declined a British request to send Russian mercenaries to fight against George Washington and his army. Russian Cossacks and mariners also continued to explore the Far East and even established a permanent settlement in Alaska in 1784.

Although Catherine had always thought of herself as a benevolent ruler, the bloody excesses of the French Revolution and a major serf rebellion at home made her increasingly distrustful of the Enlightenment ideals that had successfully guided her early reign. During the last five years of her life, she grew particularly anxious that the revolutionary contagion from France might infect the Russian people. She began to restrict freedom of speech and grew less interested in reform. Instead, she focused ever more attention on her family, particularly her grandson Alexander, whom she hoped would succeed her as czar. By 1796, Catherine was also beginning to feel her sixty-seven years. One night when a shooting star crossed the sky, she lamented, "That is a portent of my death."[37] Rising early one November morning, she suffered a massive stroke while preparing for the day's work ahead.

Through good governance, natural population growth, and conquest, by the end of her reign Catherine had almost doubled the population of the empire and increased its size by more than 200,000 square miles—an area roughly the size of France. Russia now stretched from central Europe in the west to Alaska in the east, and from subtropical Crimea in the south to the frozen Arctic Ocean in the north. She is still admired in her adopted country today for helping create a modern and powerful Russian state. Some of Russia's neighbors may remember her legacy more critically, but all peoples can be inspired by the teenage girl who arrived friendless in a foreign land and transformed herself into one of the most powerful women in human history through intellect, grit, and diligence.

37   Henri Troyat, *Catherine the Great* (New York: Penguin Group, 1994).

George Washington

George Washington was born in 1732 in rural Virginia. The praise of him as "Father of his Country" and "First in war, first in peace and first in the hearts of his countrymen" was accurate and justly deserved. Without Washington's leadership, sacrifice, and perseverance, the American Revolution would almost certainly have failed. Without Washington, the nation would almost certainly have descended into anarchy or tyranny. His leading of the Continental Army, chairing of the Constitutional Convention, and service as the nation's first president are all well known. However, many of his greatest accomplishments have been forgotten or ignored.

Despite his almost continuous public service, Washington also had a strong social life and many interests outside of politics. He was avidly engaged in business, architecture, and scientific farming at his home of Mount Vernon. He was successfully and happily married to the widow Martha Custis; during the revolution, she would travel each winter to the army's camp to share his hardships. Perhaps due to an illness in Washington's childhood, Washington and Martha never had children of their own, but Washington was a responsible and caring stepfather and uncle. He also surrounded himself with talented and energetic young men as junior officers during the war and in government. Some of these men, such as the Marquis de Lafayette and

Alexander Hamilton, became his de facto sons and remained devoted to him throughout their lives. Washington took an active interest in the well-being and moral development of this extended family, and many of his maxims come from advice he provided in private letters, in addition to his many public statements and speeches. Washington is often perceived as he's portrayed in his statues—mythological, formal, and remote—but he also had a much more likeable and human side. He enjoyed playing cards, attending parties, dancing, and riding horses at breakneck speed. Like every man, though, he was not infallible and made some significant mistakes in his career.

Washington's father died when he was eleven, and George had to take on many of the responsibilities of manhood early, largely forgoing any advanced education. At sixteen he left this home and had his first adventure, surveying land in the wilderness of western Virginia. Thus began his first career as a backwoodsman and wilderness explorer. At twenty-one he was selected to lead an expedition into the heart of the western wilderness across the Appalachian Mountains and serve the French government with an ultimatum to withdraw. Unfortunately, his youthful inexperience led him to a series of blunders in dealing with the French, which largely triggered the Seven Years' War. This is often described as the first true world war because it pitted the French against the British and their American colonies on multiple continents and oceans. Within two years, however, he had redeemed himself by saving a combined British and colonial army from total annihilation through a combination of personal bravery, energy, and initiative.

Given Washington's military record, commanding presence, and virtuous reputation, the Continental Congress turned to him almost immediately to lead the army when the American Revolution began. Washington was not a military genius, and he lost more battles than he won. However, he was able to preserve the Continental Army through eight long years of war despite facing a stronger opponent, repeated defeats, and a chronic lack of food, clothing, money, and supplies. He learned to only risk open battle when the element of surprise and superiority of numbers made victory almost certain. Washington's leadership strengths in times of trial are well illustrated by the battles of Trenton and Princeton.

By December 1776, the American Revolution was all but over, and the euphoria of the Declaration of Independence replaced by gloom. Washington and the Continental Army were outmatched and almost destroyed in a series of battles that resulted in the loss of New York City. The battered remnants of the army were chased across New Jersey, only escaping the British by retreating across the Delaware River to Pennsylvania and taking all boats to the western shore. One of Washington's generals described their force as a "shadow army," and as a senior British official described it, "The fact is their army is broken all to pieces, the spirit of their leaders and their abettors is all broken .... I think one may venture to pronounce that it is all over with them."[38] By mid-December the Continental Congress had fled the capital of Philadelphia, thinking its defense was hopeless, and in less than two weeks, more than half of the remaining solders were leaving for home as their enlistments ended. Even Washington privately confessed that "my neck does not feel as though it were made for a halter"[39] and considered moving the pitiful remnants of the army into the western wilderness to escape the vengeful British. However, he planned one last desperate "lucky blow" by recrossing the Delaware River on Christmas night in hopes of delivering a victory for the revolution. In fact, the password on the night of the attack was "victory or death."

At nightfall on Christmas Day, Washington's small force began to ferry across the river in a blinding snowstorm. Other than the shape of the boat, the famous painting by Emanuel Leutze is an accurate depiction of how it must have been that night. After a nine-mile

---

38   David McCullough, *1776* (New York: Simon and Schuster, 2005).

39   McCullough, *1776*.

march in the worsening storm, Washington and his men appeared out of the snow, catching the British garrison by surprise and achieving a much-needed victory. This was followed up by another win on January 3 at Princeton, New Jersey, where Washington was almost killed riding between the two armies to rally his men. These two relatively small battles, won by a small, ill-equipped force, likely saved the American Revolution and the cause of American independence. Washington then had to wait five years for a chance to defeat a large British army at Yorktown, with indispensable help from the French army and navy, and force the British to the negotiating table.

Almost unique in human history, Washington was able to resist the temptations and corrupting influence of absolute power. On repeated occasions, he refused to accept kingship or dictatorship when it was his for the taking. In 1782 the war was won and the Continental Army was soon to be disbanded. However, the officers and men who had put up with danger and deprivation for so long were likely to be sent home without the years of pay they were owed, and many faced poverty. The state governments and the Continental Congress refused to keep promises made during the dark days of the war and would not or could not pay. Open rebellion and civil war were likely if the army marched on the capital to demand their fair due. After Washington made it clear that he would refuse to be either a dictator or a king, the angry officers for the first time risked turning on him. At this critical moment, Washington called a meeting with the disgruntled officer corps to urge them to turn away from civil war. In front of five hundred angry men, Washington made a plea for patience and restraint. The audience was initially unmoved, until Washington, attempting to read a letter, began to search in one of his pockets. He pulled out a pair of glasses, which his men had never before seen him wear, explaining ,"Gentlemen, you will permit me to put on my spectacles, for I have not only grown grey, but almost blind in the service of my country."[40] Many of his hardened officers, reminded of the countless sacrifices their general had made, began to weep; all thoughts of mutiny ended.

In 1783, with peace secured, Washington bid a tearful goodbye to his men, resigned his commission to Congress, and returned to Mount Vernon as a private citizen. The voluntary abdication of power was almost unprecedented. As King George III of Britain is reported to have said when told of Washington's intention to give up power, "If he does that, he will be the greatest man in the world."[41]

The plantation desperately needed his attention. It had fallen into disrepair during the war as Washington spent much of his own fortune to support the army. However, Washington's quiet time at home was short lived. He was called to chair the Constitutional Convention and ultimately to serve two terms as the first president of the United States. He performed his final great act for the fragile new democracy by refusing to run for a third term. By retiring from office voluntarily and allowing another man to be elected, Washington laid a cornerstone of democratic government and avoided the all-too-common trap of becoming a president for life who will only give up power by assassination, revolution, or death. Like the Roman hero Cincinnatus, Washington freely relinquished power and returned to his beloved Mount Vernon to live out his life as a simple farmer. However, after two short years of peace, Washington caught pneumonia while riding in the hail and cold rain. He passed away in 1799 with the final words, "I die hard but I am not afraid to go – Tis well."[42]

Washington has sometimes been reproached for being a slave owner, but this criticism fails to consider his progressive actions and

---

40   Joseph J. Ellis, *His Excellency: George Washington* (New York: Alfred A. Knopf, 2004).

41   Ron Chernow, *Washington, A Life* (New York: Penguin Press, 2010).

42   James Thomas Flexner, *Washington, The Indispensable Man* (New York: Penguin Books, 1969).

ideals in the context of their time. He had become more and more troubled by slavery as his horizons expanded from an isolated tobacco farmer in rural Virginia to a national leader fighting for the concept that "all men are created equal and endowed by their creator with the unalienable rights of life, liberty and the pursuit of happiness." Initially this led him to refuse to purchase new slaves or to sell any of his slaves without their consent. Against the conventions of the time, he also allowed his slaves to permanently marry, and, when possible, he appointed black overseers. However, as the end of his life approached, Washington was increasingly troubled by the entire institution of slavery. In fact, he stated that should the union separate between North and South, "He had made up his mind to move and be of the northern."[43] Alone among the revolutionary leadership from the South, he resolved to free all his slaves. In a carefully worded will, Washington ordered all the slaves he directly owned to be freed upon his death and also included financial provisions to care for the young, old, and sickly. He hoped this would serve as an example for others to follow. Within five years of his death, all northern states and territories, with over half the country's population, had voluntarily abolished slavery; unfortunately, it took the bloody Civil War with over 600,000 deaths to end the institution of slavery in the South sixty years later.

The abolitionist work of both Franklin and Washington was revolutionary for its time. Slavery and serfdom had existed in nearly all human cultures across the world and throughout human history. It would be roughly thirty years after Washington's death before abolition had its first major global successes with the banning of slavery in the British Empire and in many former Spanish colonies. Roughly one hundred years would elapse before slavery and serfdom were abolished in most of Eastern Europe and Asia. Surprisingly, it was nearly two hundred years before slavery was belatedly abolished in

---

43   Flexner, *Washington, The Indispensable Man.*

much of the Middle East and North Africa, typically only after intense international pressure was applied to independent countries such as Turkey (1924), Ethiopia (1942), Saudi Arabia (1962), Oman (1970), and Mauritania (1981).

Johann Wolfgang von Goethe

Johann Goethe was born in 1749 in the free city of Frankfurt am Main in modern-day Germany. He is Germany's most famous author, poet, and playwright and has had as profound an influence on the modern German language as Shakespeare had upon English. He was also an accomplished statesman, scientist, philosopher, architect, and theater director. After Benjamin Franklin, he was one of the world's last true Renaissance men. Unfortunately, other than his famous epic *Faust*, about a philosopher who makes a wager with the devil in exchange for knowledge and wisdom, most of his writings are little known in English. However, his literary works created a sensation throughout Europe and helped usher in a new literary and poetic era on the continent.

Goethe lived during the waning days of the Holy Roman Empire, whose boundaries covered modern-day Germany as well as several surrounding territories. In reality, as Voltaire said, this empire was "neither holy, nor Roman, nor an empire."[44] It was a very loose collection of roughly three hundred small independent kingdoms, duchies, principalities, and democratic free cities. This was the land of fairy-tale Germany with dark evergreen forests, old medieval towns,

---

44 Voltaire, "An Essay on Universal History, the Manners, and Spirit of Nations: From the Reign of Charlemaign to the Age of Lewis XIV" (United Kingdom: J. Nourse, 1759).

and castle-topped mountains. At this time, the Brothers Grimm were beginning to collect scores of familiar German folk tales such as "Hansel and Gretel," "Sneewittchen (Snow White)," and "Rapunzel." It was the time of Mozart and Beethoven, who set many of Goethe's works to music. Traveling across this land, even by foot, one could cross into a new country almost every day, each with its own unique government, German dialect, foods, and customs. It was also an unsettled time as Germany was shaken by echoes of the French Revolution and later as Napoleon invaded and ultimately destroyed the old political order.

Over the last decades of his long life, Goethe began to jot down (on whatever paper was at hand) observations, proverbs, insights, and advice as they came to him. These were eventually collected and compiled into a book called *Maxims and Reflections*. His personal secretary, Johann Peter Eckermann, also began to record Goethe's conversations with scientists, artists, statesmen, and celebrities as they visited the famous old man during his last years and created a book titled *Conversations of Goethe*. These two works are rich sources of wisdom from a great artist who was looking back on a long, productive life.

Goethe was born into an upper-middle-class family and was educated by a series of tutors. He was a precocious student and rapidly mastered Latin, Greek, French, English, and Italian as well as his native German. His earliest surviving poem was written when he was only eight years old. His father wanted him to become a lawyer, and he was sent to study first at the university in Leipzig and later in Strasbourg. However, he did not find his classes very satisfying and was increasingly drawn to the world of poetry and the arts. He eventually graduated with a lesser degree, but one which would still allow him to practice law.

On returning home he fitfully put his legal education to work while focusing ever more on writing. He was deeply influenced by Shakespeare, who was little know in Germany at the time, and resolved to introduce the Bard's style into German literature. With the publication of *The Sorrows of Young Werther*, Goethe became one of the best-known authors in Europe. At the age of only twenty-five, he had almost single-handedly founded the "Storm and Stress" literary movement, which was more emotional and less rule-bound than older writing styles. His poetry also flourished during this period, drawing inspiration from the beauty and power of nature as well as a series of short but intense love affairs.

His fame attracted the attention of Duke Karl August from the tiny country of Saxe-Weimar-Eisenach. Goethe was invited to come live in the small capital city of Weimar, which was renowned as a center of the arts and sciences. At this time, it was described as having ten thousand poets and a few inhabitants. Goethe resolved to spend a few years there, but only if it pleased him. He never imagined that he would spend the rest of his life in this small town and the duke would grow into one of his greatest lifelong friends. Within a year of his arrival in 1775, he was appointed to the ruling council. In response to complaints about his lack of experience, the duke replied, "Not to use a man of genius at the place where he can best employ his extraordinary talents would be to misuse him."[45] Goethe spent the next ten years of his life engaged in government while writing and studying the natural sciences in his limited free time. He acted variously as fire marshal, diplomat, roads commissioner, head of the tiny five-hundred-man army, and eventually became minister of finance. Goethe threw himself into this work both as a personal test and because he felt that: "Knowledge is not enough, we must apply it. Willing is not enough, we must do."[46] He had a reputation as a thoughtful reformer who helped make meaningful improvements in the governance of the little kingdom. However, Goethe was definitely

---

45   Peter Boerner, *Goethe* (London: Haus Publishing, 2005).

46   J. W. Goethe, *Maxims and Reflections*, translated by Elizabeth Stopp, introduction by Peter Hutchinson (London: Penguin Books, 1998).

not a revolutionary like his contemporary George Washington. He believed a wise and benevolent monarch ruling with foresight in the best interest of his subjects represented the best form of government. Although he often spoke of the German Fatherland, he did not feel that Germany needed to be politically unified and was very happy with the patchwork of small countries he lived within.

By 1786 he had grown tired of his government responsibilities and grew increasingly resentful that they prevented him from pursuing his true loves in literature and science. After being granted an indefinite leave of absence by the duke, he stole away one night, almost like a fugitive, and crossed the Alps into Italy. Goethe spent the next two years immersing himself in Italian culture and art. He rediscovered his love of writing, and his output of poems, plays, and books exploded. When he crossed the Alps again and returned to Weimer, he was a new man.

Goethe returned to the ruling council with a lighter workload, which was focused on management of the local university and on directing the Weimar state theater. Within a month of his return from Italy, he met and fell in love with Christiane Vulpius. Although it was long before they were officially married, she was his close companion for the next twenty-eight years, and they had five children together. He also found a strong new friendship with the author Schiller. This began an intense artistic collaboration that lasted until Schiller's death a decade later. Another close companion was the famous geographer, explorer, and scientist Alexander von Humboldt. Goethe's scientific interests during this period were also varied and included botany, geology, physics, and anatomy. He was a passionate (though not great) scientist. Although his two most significant works, *The Theory of Colours* and *The Metamorphosis of Plants*, did influence subsequent scientific thought, they are definitely of secondary importance compared to his literary efforts.

Goethe loved to travel, but as he got older, he left Weimar less frequently. He spent more time working in his house or going for walks in the surrounding forests and mountains. However, as his fame grew, the world increasingly came to visit him. The life pictured in *Conversations of Goethe* describes a house always full of family, friends, and guests from around the world; it was an environment of stimulating conversation and beautiful art and music. Even the conqueror Napoleon felt the need to come and speak with Goethe. He also spent increasing time translating works from other languages into German and thought it was important to bridge the linguistic barriers between countries.

Even into his seventies and eighties, Goethe had a nimble mind, was an eager learner, and remained a prolific writer. As his wife, friends, and even his children passed away before him, Goethe increasingly thought of his own mortality. One last task remained to be finished. He had begun the great classic *Faust* almost sixty years before, but it still lay incomplete. He spent the last six years of his life writing part two of the epic, only finishing it a few months before his death. Once the manuscript was complete, he remarked, "My remaining days I may now consider a free gift; it is of little consequence what I now do, or whether I do anything."[47] When Goethe passed away in 1832, he uttered his last words: "more light."[48]

---

47 Johann Peter Eckermann, *Conversations with Goethe*, Revised Edition, translated by John Oxenford (London: Elibron Classics, 2005).
48 Anthony K. Jensen, "Johann Wolfgang von Goethe (1749–1832)," Internet Encyclopedia of Philosophy, accessed September 30, 2020, https://iep.utm.edu/goethe/.

Teddy Roosevelt

Theodore Roosevelt was born in 1858 in New York City. He is remembered as one of the greatest presidents of the United States, who successfully led the country through its difficult transition into the twentieth century. He was a great reformer who relentlessly rooted out corruption and brought honesty, fairness, and competency to the government of his time. He used the "bully pulpit" of the presidency to urge all citizens to lead strenuous, virtuous lives and preached that every person should be given a "square deal" based only on their character and actions. He was the greatest conservationist and protector of the environment in the history of the United States and perhaps in the world. His early recognition that modern society was causing unsustainable harm to the Earth helped lead to the founding and critical early victories of the young conservation movement. He also found the energy and time to become an accomplished naturalist, historian, author, cowboy, war hero, explorer, and statesman as well as an engaged, loving husband and father.

Roosevelt was a very sickly and frail child who was constantly plagued by severe asthma. His earliest memories were of being held and comforted by his father as he struggled to breathe. When he was twelve years old, his father issued him a life-changing challenge: "Theodore, you have the mind but you have not the body, and without the help of the body the mind cannot go as far as it should. You must make your body. It is hard drudgery to make one's body, but I know you will do it."[49] Through years of hard exercise, he slowly transformed himself into a healthy, powerful man. By the time he left home, he could out-hike all his peers, withstand extreme outdoor conditions, and win victories in the boxing ring. His other great childhood passion was the study of animals and nature. As a little boy he taught himself hunting and taxidermy, and he established the Roosevelt Museum of Natural History in his home. He took particular delight in the study of birds and as a teenager published his first of over twenty books: *Wild Birds of the Adirondacks*. Although his interests later turned to government, he never lost his love of science, nature, and the outdoors.

After graduating from college, Roosevelt married Alice Lee and began his political career in the New York State Assembly. He soon gained a reputation as a reformer who fought vigorously against the rampant corruption in both the Republican and Democratic parties. He also found time to complete a history of the naval war of 1812 to critical acclaim. As a newlywed with a baby on the way and a successful career, Roosevelt's life was off to a promising start. However, in February 1884, everything changed when he received a telegram urging him to come home at once. His daughter had just been born, but both his wife and mother lay dying. He arrived home in time to say goodbye to his mother and for Alice to die in his arms. Roosevelt wrote in his diary, "The light has gone out of my life."

Leaving his daughter in the care of his sister, Roosevelt fled from New York for one of the last frontiers left in the continental United States, the badlands of North Dakota. Here he set up a cattle ranch under the shade of cottonwood trees on the banks of the Little Missouri River. He would spend days riding, hunting, and camping alone, trying to heal himself for, as he said, "Black care rarely sits behind a

---

49 Edmund Morris, *The Rise of Theodore Roosevelt* (New York: Ballantine Books, 1980).

rider whose pace is fast enough."[50] In time, Roosevelt fell in love with the harsh, desolate beauty of the badlands. His book *Hunting Trips of a Ranchman* shows a deep connection with the wilderness around him. During grueling roundups, cattle drives, and outlaw chases, he also earned the respect of the local cowboys, gunfighters, and pioneers who had at first treated him as a typical four-eyed East Coast "dude." In return, Roosevelt also came to trust and admire the rough frontiersman so different from his wealthy, sophisticated friends and family of New York. After almost three years he was at last ready to return home but would later remember of the badlands: "It was here the romance of my life began."[51]

On returning east, Roosevelt fell in love with and married Edith Carow, an old childhood friend. He also reentered politics, becoming a civil service commissioner in Washington, a police commissioner in New York, and eventually assistant secretary of the navy. He strove to make the government more honest and efficient. He became famous for his incorruptibility and often unorthodox methods. In New York, he spent many late nights wandering the streets of the city, catching surprised police officers sleeping, shirking their duties, or accepting bribes.

Most importantly, in 1888 he founded the Boone and Crockett Club, the world's first modern conservation society. Roosevelt was an avid and, by modern standards, rapacious hunter. However, he had a strict code of sportsmanship for hunting. For example, the teddy bear was named in his honor after his refusal to shoot a chained black bear. As he watched the big game animals dwindle with each trip to the west, he grew increasingly concerned about their indiscriminate slaughter. The vast buffalo herds were gone and the few remaining animals were being hunted to extinction by commercial hunters and poachers or, as Roosevelt called them, "swinish game butchers," who

---

50   Edmund Morris, *The Rise of Theodore Roosevelt*.
51   Edmund Morris, *The Rise of Theodore Roosevelt*.

shot down whole herds, stripped them of their hides, and left acres of carcasses rotting in the sun. Meanwhile, the "wealthy criminal class" colluded with corrupt politicians to clear-cut the nation's forests for short-term profit while factories choked the nation's rivers and air with pollution. Roosevelt gathered together many of the country's premier sport hunters, scientists, and concerned politicians. Together they successfully lobbied to defend Yellowstone Park from poachers, to end commercial hunting, and to establish the country's first forest preserves.

In 1898 he was instrumental in America's early naval victories in the Spanish–American War but then abruptly quit his job to enlist as a senior officer in the 1st Volunteer Cavalry Regiment, which later became famous as the Rough Riders. At their mustering grounds in Texas, men flocked to join Teddy and to liberate Cuba. The regiment became an eclectic mix of cowboys, sheriffs, prospectors, and Indian scouts from the West with athletes, fox hunters, and polo players from the Ivy League universities of the East. Although they were only together for five months, the Rough Riders gained glory in Cuba. Under withering rifle fire from the fortified Spanish positions on the summit, Colonel Roosevelt led his regiment in the famous charge up San Juan Hill. He was the first American to reach the top; as the Rough Riders surged up behind him, the enemy fled for their lives. This disparate band of volunteers had outfought the professional armies of both Spain and the United States. Roosevelt had always longed to test himself in battle, and he described the moment as the great day of his life. He arrived home to a hero's welcome and would eventually be awarded with the Congressional Medal of Honor.

His fame catapulted him into the governorship of New York, where he once again spent his first term vigorously fighting corruption and reforming the state government. His efforts made many enemies among the state's political and business elites. They contrived to nominate him to the powerless office of vice president to get him out of the way. Roosevelt was elected in 1901 despite the objection of Senator Mark Hanna, the most powerful political insider of the day, who presciently cried, "Don't any of you realize that there's only one life between this madman and the presidency?"[52] Six months later, William McKinley was assassinated by an anarchist, the great terrorist threat of the late nineteenth and early twentieth centuries. At the age of only forty-two, Roosevelt was leader of the country, and Hanna lamented, "Now look—that damn cowboy is president of the United States."[53]

The Roosevelts entered the White House as the youngest presidential couple in history—along with six energetic, mischievous children and a menagerie of dogs, ponies, pigs, lizards, rabbits, owls, macaws, snakes, bears, roosters, and even a badger "whose temper was short but whose nature was fundamentally friendly."[54] Roosevelt himself would interrupt cabinet meetings to wrestle with his children or to admire their newest pets. The White House lawn became a great playground, and all of Washington became the scene for adventurous hikes with children, friends, senators, ambassadors, and cabinet secretaries. These walks usually led straight through whatever obstacles appeared in their path and might involve burrowing through hedges, climbing walls, scaling cliffs, or swimming the Potomac River.

Through moderate sensible reform, Roosevelt strove to protect the unregulated capitalism of his time from its own worst excesses and to break the hold of the "malefactors of great wealth" on the economy and government. He became famous as a trust buster who broke up the large monopolies that were stifling competition and concentrating power into the hands of a few men. He enacted laws to ensure that the nation had access to safe food and medicines. He intervened in the

---

52 Edmund Morris, *The Rise of Theodore Roosevelt*.
53 Edmund Morris, *The Rise of Theodore Roosevelt*.
54 Theodore Roosevelt, *An Autobiography of Theodore Roosevelt* (New York: The Macmillan Company, 1913).

bitter labor disputes of the day to ensure that the workers were given a square deal. He also had many profound conservation achievements. In all, Roosevelt protected about ten percent of the United States landmass from uncontrolled exploitation and development. He was an early proponent of sustainable development, acknowledging the right of each generation to use natural resources but stating emphatically: "I do not recognize the right to waste them, or to rob, by wasteful use, the generations to come after us."[55] He established the Forest Service to ensure timber was harvested at a sustainable rate, that forests were replanted, and that critical habitats were protected. Working with a sometimes hostile Congress, his administration established 150 new national forests, fifty-one federal bird reserves, and four game preserves; he also founded or expanded five national parks. When Congress would not cooperate, he used the newly established Antiquities Act to create eighteen national monuments by executive order. The beautiful lands he helped preserve include many of America's most beloved parks such as Grand Canyon, Yosemite, Devils Tower, Mesa Verde, Crater Lake, Muir Woods and Mount Olympus.

Roosevelt also had an aggressive foreign policy. He aided revolution in Panama and was the leading force behind the construction of the Panama Canal, which proved to be an economic boon for both North and South America. Following his policy of "speaking softly and carrying a big stick," he was not opposed to using the veiled threat of force to gain favorable negotiated terms. Conversely, he was the first American to win the Nobel Peace Prize for successfully mediating an end to the bloody Russo–Japanese War in 1905.

Roosevelt had little sympathy or patience with morally flawed people. However, he strongly believed and regularly preached that each person should be judged and treated according to their individual merits without regard to their sex, race, or religion. In this he

---

55   H. Paul Jeffers, *The Bully Pulpit: A Teddy Roosevelt Book of Quotations* (Lanham: Taylor Trade Publishing, 2002).

powerfully foreshadowed Martin Luther King Jr. who, a half century later, would dream that his children "will be judged not by the color of their skin but by the content of their character."[56] Roosevelt was an early supporter of women's equality in the workplace and the right to vote. He came to see the Indians as valiant but vanquished opponents in the struggle for the North American continent and was outraged by the subsequent breaking of treaties and their ill treatment by corrupt government officials. Early in his presidency he caused a major controversy by inviting Booker T. Washington, the eminent African-American educator, author, and civil rights leader, to the White House for dinner. Washington became an advisor to Roosevelt, who undoubtedly agreed with his vision to promote advancement for the African-American community through education and self-reliance.

In 1909, Roosevelt left the White House and was succeeded by his friend William Taft. He departed for Africa to lead a year-long combined hunting safari and scientific expedition sponsored by the Smithsonian Institute. On returning home he grew increasingly unhappy with the conservative agenda Taft was pursuing. When denied the Republican nomination in 1912, he and other reform-minded politicians broke away to form the Progressive Party. Just before delivering a campaign speech in Milwaukee, Roosevelt was shot by a would-be assassin. With the bullet still lodged in his chest, Roosevelt launched into his full speech by calling to the crowd, "Friends, I shall ask you to be as quiet as possible. I don't know whether you fully understand that I have just been shot; but it takes more than that to kill a bull moose."[57] Despite his vigorous and sometimes heroic efforts on the campaign trail, he lost his bid for the presidency. As before,

---

56   Martin L. King, "I Have a Dream," speech presented at the March on Washington for Jobs and Freedom, Washington, D.C., August 1968, http://avalon.law.yale.edu/20th_century/mlk01.asp.

57   John Gabriel Hunt, *The Essential Theodore Roosevelt* (New York: Gramercy Books, 1994).

when feeling the sting of sorrow or disappointment, Teddy plunged into a new adventure. This time he led an expedition to float down the unexplored and unmapped "River of Doubt" in the Amazonian jungles of Brazil. The expedition severely tested the aging Roosevelt, who became deathly ill and at one point demanded that his son and friends leave him behind so they could reach safety. In the end, the battered and sickened group did emerge from the jungle. They had succeeded in mapping a new five-hundred-mile-long river system, which was subsequently renamed the Rio Teodoro, but Roosevelt's health never recovered.

When the United States entered World War I in 1917, all four of Roosevelt's boys volunteered and fought bravely. However, the fierce, grinding warfare in the trenches of France was very different to the brief, glorious charge up San Juan Hill. The bloody, senseless war, accidentally sparked by the assassination of Austria's enlightened crown prince by a Serbian assassin, also bore little resemblance to the crusade to end Spain's often brutal colonial rule in Cuba. In 1918, Roosevelt's youngest son, Quentin, was shot down during a combat flight over France. Quentin's death broke Roosevelt's heart. His body was also breaking down. The bullet from Milwaukee was still in his chest, and malaria from the River of Doubt expedition continued to plague him. Just after his sixtieth birthday, he was told he might never be able to walk again, but refusing to despair, he immediately replied, "All right, I can work that way too."[58] Within months he died in his sleep. His surviving sons, still serving in Europe, received the sad news by telegram: "The old lion is dead."[59]

Theodore Roosevelt's greatest legacy is undoubtedly his help in the establishment of the modern environmental movement and the preservation of so many of North America's natural treasures. But

---

58   Candice Millard, *The River of Doubt: Theodore Roosevelt's Darkest Journey* (New York: Anchor Books, 2005).
59   Candice Millard, *The River of Doubt*.

he would likely have been most proud of his six children, to whom he had devoted so much love and energy. Almost all led successful and influential lives. His eldest son, Ted, even earned the Congressional Medal of Honor in World War II for his bravery and skill as the first general ashore during the D-Day landings in 1944.

George Washington Carver

George Washington Carver was born in 1864 on a small farm in Missouri. Born into slavery and orphaned as a baby, he became a famous agricultural scientist due in part to his brilliance and passion for learning. As a professor at Tuskegee University in Alabama, he trained and inspired a generation of black teachers and specialists who worked to raise subsistence farmers out of extreme poverty across the American South. He was an early proponent of sustainable agriculture and careful preservation of the country's soil resources. Carver's scientific accomplishments, exceptional oratory skills, and ability to make deep friendships with influential whites helped expose the illogic and injustice of segregation. The work of Carver, along with other talented black professionals in the military, sports, sciences, and arts led to major improvements in race relations in the 1940s, fully two decades before the more celebrated civil rights victories of the 1960s.

More than thirty million men and women may have been taken from the African continent during many centuries of slave raids and coastal trading. It is likely that over half of these Africans were enslaved in the Middle East and almost all of the others were sold into Latin America and the Caribbean. George Washington Carver was a descendant of the roughly two percent of enslaved Africans who were brought to colonial North America. Although born a slave,

Carver was freed as a baby by Missouri's abolition law and the 13th Amendment of 1865. In the chaotic days at the end of the Civil War, Carver, his sister, and their mother were kidnapped from the farm where they lived. His former owner hired a Union cavalry scout to recover the stolen family, but only young George was found. The childless Carvers raised George as their own. He was a sickly child and was mostly given light chores around the house to earn his keep.

The Carvers soon realized that he had an especially curious and active mind. They taught him to read and gave him time to ponder nature in the fields and forests around the farm. George's knowledge soon outstripped that of his white foster parents, and at the age of twelve he started attending a small school about eight miles away. This began a quest for learning that was to span twenty years and lead Carver across Missouri, Kansas, and Iowa. At many schools he quickly learned all the teachers had to offer and had to look for new challenges. At others he was turned away because of the color of his skin. During this period, Carver used the skills he had learned from his foster parents to support himself. He would often set up a laundry service, do house chores for room and board, or act as a farmhand. Finally, at the age of about twenty-six, Carver was able to realize his dream of higher education. He first enrolled in the art program at Simpson College in Iowa but later transferred to the Iowa State Agricultural College.

Carver was the only African American at both schools, but his sharp mind and gentle character rapidly earned him many friends and admirers. At Iowa State he showed a particular talent for botany and mycology (the study of fungi). He also continued to paint and even had his work exhibited at the Chicago World's Fair of 1893, where it received an honorable mention. Carver eventually received both a bachelor's and master's degree in agriculture from Iowa State, and he also began to teach there. He was now one of the most highly educated African-Americans in the United States. He had a good position at Iowa State and doubtless could have completed his PhD there. However, when Booker T. Washington offered him the chance to teach at the Tuskegee Institute, he could not decline the chance to help "his people."

Tuskegee was founded as a school for teachers in 1881 and rapidly became one of the foremost centers for black education in the United States. It was purposefully located in the center of the impoverished cotton belt of Alabama. In 1896, Carver was appointed as both the director of agriculture at Tuskegee and the director of the affiliated State Agriculture Experiment Station. He was likely shocked on many levels when he arrived in Alabama. The soils and farmlands in the region were deeply eroded and severely depleted by decades of mismanaged cotton monoculture. It was also his first time in the Deep South, and he may not have expected the intense bigotry he initially encountered. Lastly, he had spent most of his life working with and befriending whites from the Midwest, so he had some difficulty relating to the other black faculty members at the campus.

Most of Carver's time was devoted to teaching and mentoring the students at Tuskegee. He was universally acknowledged as a great technical teacher who could also motivate and inspire his students. He also firmly believed that education should improve the morality and character of his pupils, not just provide them with a trade. This occurred both in the formal classrooms but also in a weekly Bible class that he led for decades. Carver was much less successful as a college administrator, perhaps because he had to spend so much time teaching and doing agricultural research.

It had only been a few decades since the German chemist Justus von Liebig had first applied scientific methods to agricultural problems. Liebig had clearly demonstrated the importance of soil nutrients, particularly nitrogen, to successful farming outcomes. Carver immediately started to apply these new agricultural theories to the practical problems of the South. He searched for ways to build up the worn-out local soils for, as he put it, "whenever the soil is wasted, the people are wasted."[60] He began a lifelong quest to find and promote crops that would help replenish the soil while also providing nourishment to the poor farmers and their families. He eventually found three nitrogen-fixing plants to focus his attention on: peanuts, cow peas, and sweet potatoes. He also began work on agricultural practices such as crop rotation and use of free naturally available fertilizers that could be used by "the man furthest down." Carver had to perform this work on a paltry budget and with almost no help. To outfit his first laboratory, he scoured the local landfill for old bottles and jars, and he had to make many of his reagents himself. To promote his practical solutions, Carver wrote over forty widely read agricultural bulletins during his career. To make the publications more pertinent, he typically wrote simple cultivation instructions for farmers, a summary of botanical characteristics for teachers, and recipes for cooks.

Over time, his career became more and more focused on the issues of peanut production, for which he later became famous. He helped solve disease problems to enhance crop yield, worked with processing companies to improve efficiencies, and became a spokesman to promote peanut consumption. In 1921, this effort culminated in his celebrated appearance before the United States House of Representatives, where he argued for tariffs to protect the fledgling industry. He also began to lecture at local farmers meetings and conferences to spread the message of sustainable scientific agriculture. Carver displayed a remarkable talent for public speaking, for making his topics accessible to his audience, and for inspiring action. He started being invited to speaking engagements at conferences, fairs, and meetings across the South and eventually as far away as New England.

Newspapers began to award him with names like "the Wizard of Tuskegee," and his fame grew outside of the agricultural community.

---

60   Mark Hersey, *My Work Is That of Conservation: An Environmental Biography of George Washington Carver* (Athens, Georgia: University of Georgia Press, 2011).

Carver also began to receive honors from organizations as varied as the Royal Society, the National Association for the Advancement of Colored People (NAACP), and the United Daughters of the Confederacy. Carver had a knack for making close friendships that crossed racial boundaries wherever he went in the country. Carver never married and seemed to devote all of his emotional energy to his students and the people he met during his travels. He was a prolific letter writer and maintained close contacts with hundreds of people. Some, such as the great industrialist Henry Ford and Secretary of Agriculture James Wilson, occupied positions of substantial influence. Although he was not a strident civil rights advocate, Carver's dignity in the face of discrimination when traveling had a strong effect on public opinion. A visit or lecture was commonly followed by articles on the injustice of segregation in the local and sometimes national press.

In the last five years of his life, Carver's health began to decline, hampering his research efforts and limiting his travel schedule. Thinking of his legacy, he focused his remaining energy on the creation of the Carver Research Foundation to support agricultural science studies at Tuskegee. He had always been an exceptionally frugal man and donated all of his savings accumulated over forty years of work at the university. Carver died in 1943, just two years after the foundation was established; it still exists today.

It has become a common complaint that George Washington Carver's reputation outstripped his scientific accomplishments. He only received three patents, and almost none of his inventions became commercially viable. However, this criticism misses his major contributions in other areas. He was always primarily concerned with disseminating recent agricultural advances to poor farming communities and providing practical solutions that could be adopted by those with few resources. Despite the lack of funding, he made real contributions in mycology and botany, mostly as a collaborator with other scientists. His skills as an educator helped create a generation of teachers for black schools across the American South. His fame and character also helped improve race relations across the country. Carver's quiet excellence and perseverance—much like that of the Tuskegee Airmen, the Navy's Golden Thirteen, and the baseball player Jackie Robinson—earned the respect of the broader population and shifted white public opinion on race relations. These men directly contributed to the end of segregation in the United States military, professional sports, and many other professions in the 1940s.

Mahatma Gandhi

Mohandas Gandhi was born in 1869 in the provincial town of Porbandar in western India. He was the leader of the independence movement that eventually freed India from British rule in 1947. He almost single-handedly invented the concept of nonviolent civil disobedience and mass protest that was later adopted by Martin Luther King Jr. of the United States and many later struggles for freedom, fairness, or equality. Less well known but equally important were Gandhi's efforts to reform India itself, especially his struggles to end the intense discrimination in Hindu society against Untouchables and his ultimately unsuccessful efforts to promote Hindu–Muslim unity. Gandhi was unusual in modern times as he tried to act both in the political and spiritual world simultaneously, which he thought were inseparably linked. Despite his political power, he lived a life of renunciation and poverty in the long tradition of Hindu holy men.

Gandhi grew up at the height of the British Empire, which had ruled much of India for almost a century. British conquest and capable administration had brought relative peace and prosperity to the subcontinent. The colonial government eradicated the ancient Thuggee cult, which practiced ritual murder in honor of the goddess Kali, banned female infanticide, and suppressed the practice of suttee in which widows were expected to burn alive on their husband's funeral pyre. Britain's finances and trade benefited substantially from its rule of India, but imperial India was also enriched by many new schools, hospitals, railroads, and factories. In 1858 Queen Victoria proclaimed that all her subjects in India would "enjoy the equal and impartial protection of the law" and stated that "in their prosperity will be our strength, in their contentment our security and in their gratitude our best reward."[61] However, the British soldiers and administrators often failed to put Victoria's noble words into practice: racism and paternalism were commonplace and few native Indians were allowed to hold positions of power in the colonial government. By Gandhi's sixteenth birthday, a group of well-educated and wealthy but frustrated Indians had founded the Indian National Congress to press for greater freedom, respect, and opportunity within the empire.

Gandhi was born into a relatively wealthy upper caste Hindu home. He was a shy, quiet child raised in a very traditional religious family. At the age of eighteen he left home and moved to London to study the law. There he also became a committed vegetarian and began his lifelong quest for spiritual enlightenment. Surprisingly, it was in London, not India, where some English friends first introduced him to the great Hindu text, the Bhagavad Gita. Upon graduation, Gandhi had difficulty establishing his law practice in India and so accepted a one-year legal assignment in South Africa. He would spend the next twenty years of his life there. He became a prominent member of the small but rapidly growing Indian immigrant community.

It was here that Gandhi first felt the sting of racism and discrimination. As a well-educated Indian, he was dismayed to be treated as a second-class citizen by colonial authorities and business owners. Shortly after arriving in Africa, Gandhi was thrown out of his first-class compartment on a train because a European refused to

---

61   Queen Victoria, "Proclamation by the Queen in Council to the Princes, Chiefs and people of India," Allahabad, India, November 1, 1858.

sit with a "colored man." This occurred again and again as he was denied service in hotels, restaurants, and in the law courts; he was even pushed off of sidewalks, which were reserved for whites. He was particularly incensed that sophisticated Indians, who shared a common heritage with other Indo-European peoples, were treated the same as uneducated native Africans merely because of the color of their skin. He resolved to fight for the rights and freedoms of the Indian community in South Africa in the law courts and in civil disobedience campaigns.

His protest campaigns started tentatively as he slowly developed the tactics, philosophy, and organizational skills that would lead to later successes. The ancient Indian concept of ahimsa, or non-harming, was central to Gandhi's philosophy and actions. He also gained insight from his reading of the American author Henry David Thoreau, who professed that civil disobedience was a necessary response to immoral or unjust laws; the great Russian author and pacifist Leo Tolstoy, who stressed that love and nonviolence can overcome hatred and brute force; and the example of the suffragettes of Britain, who were already practicing civil disobedience in their quest for the women's vote. His intimate knowledge of British military power likely also convinced him that violent insurrection would be doomed to failure. However, this was not an easy path. Gandhi asked himself and his followers to accept months of hard work, economic loss, jail sentences, beatings, and in rare cases even death without returning violence with violence.

Gandhi's "satyagraha" or "truth force" tactics required great personal bravery, sacrifice, and self-restraint. However, key to its success was also that the British believed in the rule of law and a sense of fair play, which left them open to moral persuasion. In almost all his battles, Gandhi had significant allies on the side of the British people and government; he just needed to persuade enough people to reach a tipping point. It is notable that such movements have had the most success in former English colonies. In retrospect, Gandhi's advice for

European Jews to practice passive resistance during the Holocaust is preposterous, just as it would have been for victims of the murderous government of World War I Turkey, the brutal Russian and Asian communist regimes of the twentieth century, or the perpetrators of intertribal genocide in Rwanda and South Sudan of Africa more recently.

Even while Gandhi was confronting unjust laws and practices, he also retained a respect for and loyalty to the empire. He built a thriving law practice in Durban and then Johannesburg during these years of protest. Even more remarkable, in 1899 he organized and led an ambulance corps that supported the British Army as it conquered the independent Boer Republics founded by the descendants of Dutch settlers who had lived in Southern Africa for centuries. In fact, both Churchill and Gandhi were to participate on the same side in one of the pivotal battles of that war. Later Gandhi would again organize an ambulance corps for the empire's war with the native Zulu tribes. He hoped to show that the Indians of South Africa were brave and worthy subjects of the queen who deserved equal rights within the empire. Unfortunately, he was to be disappointed again and again as promises made were not kept. He also gained the hostility of many native Africans who to this day remember that he did not fight for their rights but instead remained steadfastly focused on the well-being of his fellow Indians alone.

In his struggles for the Indian community, he also disappointed his family. He had entered into an arranged marriage at the age of thirteen and had four sons. However, he spent most of his time away from his family despite the complaints of his brother and children about the neglect of his duties as a husband and parent. His family life became more and more peripheral as, like the Buddha before him, he focused more of his time and energy on spiritual and political goals. In South Africa he took a vow of celibacy, began to dress as a simple Hindu peasant, and renounced most other worldly possessions

110

and pleasures. However, he and his wife remained loyal to each other until her death decades later in India.

Gandhi's first great political success came in 1913 when the government of South Africa tried to impose a heavy tax targeting Indians in an attempt to drive them out of the country. This victory came about in part because Gandhi realized he needed to mobilize all Indians, not just the well-off men but also women and the poor working class. He called a strike, which resulted in widespread walk-outs by Indian coal workers and farm laborers. Other protest actions resulted in almost seven thousand Indians being jailed. The European press supported the strikers, and portions of the local economy ground to a halt. Eventually the government had to capitulate and the hated tax was abolished.

Shortly after this first great success, Gandhi boarded a ship for India. He was already famous for his efforts in South Africa and for the publication of his book titled *Hind Swaraj* or *Indian Self-Rule*, which called for the expulsion of the British Empire from India by nonviolent means. Churchill understood the implications of this revolutionary proposal, stating that if the Indian masses refused to cooperate, "the game would be up" and "the whole thing [the empire] would collapse."[62] It was soon after his return to India that Gandhi was first called by the title of "Mahatma" or "great soul." He began to implement his strategy of satyagraha on a small scale in individual provinces to address local grievances. However, within six years he had also taken control of the Indian National Congress and gotten it to adopt his policies of nonviolence to end British rule on a national scale.

This began almost thirty years of struggle between the forces of Indian nationalism and the colonial government. The weapons on Gandhi's side included boycotts, marches, strikes, fasts, and a general refusal to cooperate with the authorities. The empire fought back with

---

62   Arthur Herman, *Gandhi and Churchill* (New York: Bantam Dell, 2008).

limited concessions, police actions, imprisonment, and sometimes violence. Gandhi spent years in jail, though typically under comfortable conditions. At times there were also tens of thousands of his followers in prison. In 1930 he launched his most widespread and iconic campaign, the famous Salt March. In protest of a tax on salt, he gathered a small group of devoted followers who were fully committed to the principles of nonviolence and marched 400 kilometers to the sea. There, in violation of the law, he defiantly gathered salt for himself and set all of India into protest, making it virtually ungovernable.

To the frustration of his supporters, Gandhi called off many of the protest campaigns when they flared into anarchy or violence. He also focused much of his time and energy trying to improve Indian society, in part to make it worthy of self-rule. Chief among these efforts was his fight against the scourge of untouchability. More than ten percent of the Indian people were considered so impure that any contact with them was intolerable to other Hindus. They were restricted to the most menial and degrading work, could not talk to or even approach high caste Hindus, had almost no legal rights, and in many cases were legally tied to the land just as slaves or serfs were. Gandhi described untouchability as "this great and indelible crime."[63] He and the brilliant untouchable leader Dr. Ambedkar worked throughout the early twentieth century for the community's rights. At Gandhi's insistence, untouchable equality became a formal goal of the Indian National Congress. At rallies and speeches, Gandhi would always preferentially seek out the local untouchable participants and in a very public manner talk, sit, and eat with them. To the horror of his wife and other traditional Hindus, whom he described as being surrounded by a "wall of prejudice,"[64] he even invited Untouchables to live in his home as equals. At times his ethical stand on equality for all Indians risked fracturing the independence movement.

---

63 Joseph Lelyveld, *Great Soul* (New York: Vintage Books, 2012).
64 Lelyveld, *Great Soul*.

Hindu–Muslim cooperation was another of Gandhi's core tenets. Over ten percent of Indians were Muslims, and there had long been tension between the two religious communities. As the Indian National Congress came to be seen as beholden to the Hindu majority, Indian Muslims increasingly turned to the Muslim League to fight for their interests. Throughout the 1920s and 1930s, as the grip of British rule weakened, violent clashes between the two religious communities escalated. Gandhi expended much of his political capital trying to maintain harmony between the two groups whom he viewed as inseparably linked.

Other worthy causes that Gandhi championed included economic self-sufficiency, women's rights, and improved public sanitation and hygiene. Gandhi produced a wealth of advice on these and many other topics in countless speeches, letters, and newspaper articles. Unfortunately, he also campaigned for other less worthy goals. Until his death he remained steadfastly opposed to vaccination, birth control, modern medicine, and industrialization, which he thought of as evils of the Western world.

With the advent of World War II, Gandhi even tried to act as an international peacemaker. In two letters to Hitler, he presciently argued, "You are leaving no legacy to your people of which they can feel proud. They cannot take pride in a recital of cruel deeds, however skillfully planned. I, therefore, appeal to you in the name of humanity to stop the war."[65] Throughout the war, even as millions of Indians agreed to fight one last time for the empire, the independence movement also made colonial rule increasingly difficult and ineffective. By 1945, the exhausted British government and people came to see continued rule in India as an unsustainable burden. Even the previously loyal Indian armed forces were beginning to mutiny, law and order was breaking down, and communal violence was spreading.

---

[65] Mahatma Gandhi, "To Adolf Hitler," accessed October 5, 2020, Gandhi Book Center, www.mkgandhi.org/mynonviolence/chap60.htm.

Independence negotiations failed, not only because of disagreements with the British, but also because the different Indian leaders and religious communities could not agree on how to share power.

Finally, in 1947, a new imperial viceroy was sent to India with orders to end British rule by any means and as rapidly as possible. By this time Gandhi was no longer central to the negotiations or involved in the big decisions. He had lost power to other politicians such as Nehru and Jinnah, who despised each other and set the country on course for partition along religious lines. Ironically, he may have wrecked the last chance for a peaceful settlement between Hindus and Muslims because he refused to sanction any religious separation. He now voluntarily retreated from politics out of frustration and to focus on quelling the violence between the two religious groups, which was spinning out of control. Mass murder, rape, forced conversion, and ethnic cleansing were increasing across the country.

Gandhi moved first to Calcutta, an epicenter of the violence, and pleaded for the two communities to put down their weapons. He faced down angry mobs and repeated death threats to little avail. Finally, entering a fast and threatening his own death, he forced the religious leaders to intervene and end the carnage. He tried to repeat this miracle of Calcutta in other locations, but he was only one man and the violence stretched across a subcontinent. When India finally received independence in August 1947, he refused to participate in any of the celebrations, even as a guest of honor. In the end, at least one million Indians died fighting each other at independence and over ten million were driven from their homes. Gandhi felt lost and a failure. He also had a premonition that he was to die a violent death as fundamentalist Muslims and Hindus both hated him.

In the end it was a Hindu nationalist who shot Gandhi down during a prayer meeting in 1948. He died with the name of the Hindu God Rama on his lips. In death Gandhi accomplished what he could not in life. Perhaps in shame, the violence across India and Pakistan rapidly subsided. Discrimination against Untouchables was outlawed in the new Indian constitution. The conditions of Untouchables today, now called Dalits, is steadily improving. India has the world's largest and one of its most vibrant democracies. Although Pakistan and India still share a tense border guarded by nuclear weapons, the violence of independence has never been repeated. The subcontinent owes much of this to the uncompromising moral guidance and example provided by Mahatma Gandhi. As Albert Einstein said, "Generations to come will scarce believe that such a man as this one ever in flesh and blood walked upon this Earth."[66]

---

66   Alice Calaprice, *The Ultimate Quotable Einstein* (Princeton: Princeton University Press, 2011).

Winston Churchill

Winston Churchill was born in 1874 at Blenheim Palace in central England. He is often described as the greatest Englishman who ever lived. As a soldier, member of Parliament, administrator, and eventually prime minister, Churchill helped guide the nation through a turbulent and dangerous half century with civil unrest, economic dislocation, two world wars, and the threat of nuclear holocaust. He has been one of history's strongest advocates for a free and democratic society. He almost single-handedly convinced the British people to fight the Nazi regime in Germany when all the rest of western and central Europe had been converted or conquered and Britain stood alone. Without his courage and strong moral conviction, the United Kingdom would almost certainly have entered into a negotiated peace, leaving Hitler victorious and totalitarian governments stretching continuously across the world from Fascist Spain and Vichy France on the Atlantic to Communist Russia and Imperialist Japan on the Pacific.

Churchill's accomplishments as an author and an artist are less well known today but would make him famous in their own right. He wrote over forty popular books mostly covering current events, history, and biography. In 1953 he won the Nobel Prize for Literature for "his mastery of historical and biographical description as well

116

as for brilliant oratory in defending exalted human values."[67] He somehow found time to write even as a leading member of Parliament or heading important departments in the British government. Unlike today's politicians, he also wrote all of his own speeches, articles, and books. This usually involved dictating to a succession of devoted but overworked secretaries between other important business during the workday. Perhaps even more surprising is that Churchill found time to paint. He took up painting to relieve the stress of politics and war. He loved to paint landscapes in bright colors, usually in an Impressionist style. His paintings were praised in his lifetime and are still displayed in many international art museums. Even Pablo Picasso, who disliked Churchill's politics, begrudgingly admitted that he would have been a very successful artist if he took up painting as a profession.

Despite the demands of his career, Churchill also had a strong and loving family life. He was married to his beloved Clementine for fifty-seven years and they had five children together. Churchill's kindness also extended to his many pets, including a menagerie of ducks, geese, cats, dogs, fish, and pigs. He famously said, "Dogs look up to you, cats look down on you. Give me a pig! He looks you in the eye and treats you as an equal."[68] Like Teddy Roosevelt, Churchill was considered a very talented but eccentric character who dressed and spoke in an archaic manner. He was renowned for his biting wit, which he deployed during Parliamentary debates and at social events. He was rarely to be seen without his trademark cigar and glass of whiskey in hand throughout the day.

Churchill had a difficult childhood with few close friends, a distant mother, and an unkind, sometimes cruel father. Young Winston was not good in school and usually ended each year near the bottom of

---

67 "The Nobel Prize in Literature 1953," NobelPrize.org, accessed October 5, 2020, www.nobelprize.org/prizes/literature/1953/summary/.
68 Richard Langworth, *Churchill by Himself: The Definitive Collection of Quotations* (New York: Public Affairs, 2008).

his class. It was not until he attended Sandhurst, Britain's military academy, that he finally began to show some measure of his later brilliance and drive. He graduated in 1894, near the peak of the British Empire's power and majesty.

His early military career reads like a Victorian adventure novel. During this period he first showed the great personal and moral courage that was a trademark of his whole life. He volunteered and fought in the remote mountains of India's northwest frontier against wild Afghan tribesman. Next, he joined the 21st Lancers in time for their famous cavalry charge in the Battle of Omdurman in Sudan. Four hundred British horsemen charged over 2,500 enemy infantrymen and drove them from the field. Churchill was in the middle of the melee firing his pistol into the packed enemy at close range. His last colonial adventure was during the Boer War in South Africa, where he was taken prisoner. Upon making a heroic escape, he returned to Britain as a celebrated war hero. Like Teddy Roosevelt, he used this to launch his political career.

He was first elected to Parliament in 1900 and served almost continuously for sixty-four years. He was deeply devoted to the institution and became one of its staunchest advocates and defenders. Within five years he also began a career as a government minister, which included posts like home secretary, first lord of the Admiralty, secretary for air and war, colonial secretary, chancellor of the exchequer (the second most powerful office in the British government), and finally prime minister. During his long and varied service before World War II, he helped shape the world we have inherited. He was responsible for negotiating Irish independence from Britain and was one of the prime supporters of a Jewish homeland in then British-ruled Palestine. Conversely, he remained a firm believer in the British Empire as a force for good, even as many of its subjects tired of British paternalism and yearned for freedom and self-rule. Churchill argued strongly against

Indian independence and intensely disliked Mahatma Gandhi, one of the twentieth century's most admired figures.

During World War I he was the leading proponent in the invention of the tank and the development of an air force. He was also an avid pioneer flyer himself at a time when it was still extremely dangerous. In fact, Churchill had a reputation not only for bravery but also for being rash and somewhat unsteady. Perhaps his worst failure occurred during World War I at the Battle of Gallipoli in Turkey. As bloody trench warfare raged in France, Churchill searched for a way to break the stalemate and end the carnage. He became the prime proponent of a bold plan to force the straights between the Mediterranean and the Black Sea, make Turkey surrender, and establish a supply line to Britain's ally Russia. Unfortunately, the operation was poorly planned and badly mismanaged by the admirals and generals in the field. It became a costly fiasco, borne mostly by Australian and New Zealand troops. To this day Churchill is not well-liked in either country. This disaster forced him to leave the Admiralty; in characteristic fashion, he then volunteered to serve with the army in the trenches of France.

He was also out of favor with senior government leaders through-out the 1930s, a period that has been called his "wilderness years." He spent much of this period as a lonely voice in Parliament warning of the dangers posed by the new Fascist governments in Spain, Italy, Eastern Europe, and—above all—Germany. His warnings fell on deaf ears. Many in Britain before World War II admired the Nazis for successfully raising their country out of starvation, hopelessness, and economic depression, and for acting as a bulwark against the Communists. The British people were also tired of war, and many felt guilty about the harsh and unjust Treaty of Versailles, which had been imposed upon Germany, Austria, and Hungary at the end of the First World War. One senior British general at the time presciently called it "the peace to end all peace."[69]

However, this all changed when German Blitzkrieg (lightning war) raced across Holland, Belgium, and France in just six weeks in 1940. France was beaten and the British Army was humiliated and almost destroyed. In this hour of need, Churchill become prime minister, in large part because no one else wanted the job. Most people felt it would involve either overseeing a total military defeat or negotiating a disastrous peace treaty with Hitler, confirming his supremacy in Europe. The mood in the government was for surrender. Much to his cabinet's surprise, Churchill refused, stating, "If this long island story of ours is to end at last, let it end only when each one of us lies choking in his own blood upon the ground."[70] His resolve convinced the skeptical cabinet to fight on, and in a series of later speeches to Parliament and the British people, he stirred the nation to stand alone and fight through to victory through five long years of war. His vision laid out in the dark days of June 1940 came true:

> The whole fury and might of the enemy must very soon be turned on us. Hitler knows that he will have to break us in this island or lose the war. If we can stand up to him, all Europe may be free and the life of the world may move forward into broad, sunlit uplands. But if we fail, then the whole world, including the United States, including all that we have known and cared for, will sink into the abyss of a new Dark Age made more sinister, and perhaps more protracted, by the lights of perverted science. Let us therefore brace ourselves to our duties, and so bear ourselves that, if the British Empire and its Commonwealth last for a thousand years, men will still say, "This was their finest hour."[71]

---

69   David Fromkin, *A Peace to End All Peace* (New York: Henry Holt, 1989).

70   Boris Johnson, *The Churchill Factor: How One Man Made History* (New York: Riverhead Books, 2014).

71   Richard Langworth, *Churchill by Himself: The Definitive Collection of Quotations* (New York: Public Affairs, 2008).

Once the danger to Britain had passed, the war entered a new phase as the Allied armies of Britain, the United States, and the Soviet Union began "Closing the Ring" around the Axis powers. Churchill, eager to go on the offensive, has been accused of brutality for the indiscriminate terror bombing of German cities toward the end of the war, which resulted in over half a million civilian deaths. In his desperation to hold back a Japanese invasion, he also refused to divert resources away from the war effort, delaying needed food shipments and contributing to more than two million deaths in the great Bengal (modern-day Bangladesh) famine of 1943.

As the war drew to a close, he also began to warn the American government and the British people about the danger posed by Joseph Stalin and the Soviets. However, the nation was exhausted, and in the election of 1945, his political opponents won a landslide victory under the slogan "Cheer Churchill – Vote Labour." Clementine, trying to find some good from the defeat, said, "It may be a blessing in disguise," to which Winston replied, "At the moment it seems quite effectively disguised."[72] He retreated to his country home at Chartwell and traveled to the south of France to lose himself in painting and writing. However, he remained in Parliament and eventually became prime minister again from 1951 to 1955. During this postwar period he continued to warn against the new tyranny being imposed on Eastern Europe by the Soviet Red Army. It was Churchill who coined the term "Iron Curtain" to describe the Soviet occupation and in the same speech decried the largest episode of ethnic cleansing in human history: the brutal displacement of more than ten million ethnic Germans from their ancestral homes in Eastern Europe. He was also one of the first to speak of the need for a "United States of Europe" and to this day is considered one of the founding fathers of the European Union. Eventually, aware of the existential danger

---

72   Langworth, *Churchill by Himself.*

posed by nuclear weapons, Churchill also became one of the first and strongest voices calling for détente with the Soviet Union in order to prevent an accidental nuclear war.

When he was eighty-nine, Churchill made his last visit to the House of Commons, silently bowing to the speaker's chair at his departure. He died the next year in 1965. No man had left a stronger mark on the twentieth century. His life can be well summarized with his own words: "Withhold no sacrifice, grudge no toil, seek no sordid gain, fear no foe. All will be well."[73]

---

73 Langworth, *Churchill by Himself.*

MAXIMS

A maxim is a short statement of a fundamental principle, truth, or rule for living. The wisdom of these eighteen sages is captured in over eight hundred of their maxims grouped into roughly seventy themes. These themes are ordered alphabetically from *acceptance* to *work-life balance* and are intended to capture the most important aspects of a flourishing life. May this timeless wisdom bring you as much insight, success, and happiness as it has brought to countless people before us.

🙶 Acceptance

*Live in peace with what you have and what
the Gods give will come naturally.*
−Ptah-Hotep

*You should not scorn what you have received,
nor live envying what others have.*
−Buddha

*Let fate find us ready and strong. The noble spirit puts itself in the
hands of the Gods while the petty and worthless man will not
accept his fate. Instead he sees nothing good in the ordering of the
universe and prefers to reform the Gods rather than himself.*
−Seneca

*It is not the man who has too little who is poor,
but the man who always craves more.*
−Seneca

*A man must grow accustomed to his conditions, complain as little
as possible, and grasp whatever good lies within his reach.*
−Seneca

*It is always and everywhere within your power to be
content with what the Gods have given you.*
−Marcus Aurelius

Be thankful for your gifts, however humble.
−Marcus Aurelius

*Do not covet the gifts which God has given
to some men more than others.*
—Muhammad

The past cannot be cured.
—Elizabeth

Who is rich? He who rejoices in his portion.
—Franklin

Blessed is he who expects nothing, for he shall never be disappointed.
—Franklin

*One should see and think of the beauty in
everything. Let no one complain.*
—Catherine

*It is not for man to scan the wisdom of Providence.
The best he can do is to submit to its decrees.*
—Washington

*Who is the wisest of men? He who neither knows nor
wishes for anything other than what happens.*
—Goethe

*The least gifted man can be complete if he acts within
the limits of his capabilities and skills.*
—Goethe

*There is nothing more foolish and cowardly than to be beaten
down by sorrow which nothing we can do will change.*
—Roosevelt

A lady or gentleman neither looks up to the rich or down on the poor.
—Carver

How often in life must one be content with what one can get.
—Churchill

Action

To see what is right and not to do it shows a lack of courage.
—Confucius

*Virtue is not upheld by talking about it. Virtue is
upheld by living in harmony with it.*
—Buddha

*Learning about virtue is not enough; we must also strive
to be virtuous or else all our learning is useless.*
—Aristotle

*Never are all options so blocked off that there
is no room left for honorable action.*
—Seneca

*A good man will do what he thinks is honorable, even if it requires
great effort, even if it will hurt him, and even if it is dangerous.*
—Seneca

Stop theorizing about what it is to be a good man and become one!
—Marcus Aurelius

*Without clarity, decisiveness has no way of working;
without decisiveness, clarity has no place to work.*
—Zhu Xi

Let us not, nor do you, consult so long that advice comes too late.
—Elizabeth

Do more, prattle less.
—Catherine

Criticism is easy, but art is difficult.
—Catherine

Knowledge is not enough, we must apply it.
Willing is not enough, we must do.
—Goethe

How can a man get to know himself—not by thinking but by doing.
Try to do your duty and you will soon discover what you are worth.
—Goethe

It is not the critic who counts, not the man who points out how the strong man stumbled or where the doer of deeds could have done better. The credit belongs to the man who is actually in the arena.
—Roosevelt

It is hard to fail, but it is worse never having tried to succeed.
—Roosevelt

Action expresses priorities.
—Gandhi

Deeds are better than words.
—Gandhi

Criticism is easy; achievement is more difficult.
—Churchill

There is great hope provided action is taken worthy of the opportunity.
—Churchill

Addiction and Self-Control

It is harmful to take pleasure in showing off, in frivolous enjoyments and in a self-indulgent life.
—Confucius

Those driven by fierce desires are like a spider caught in its own web.
—Buddha

The person lacking discipline knows his actions are bad, but is impelled to do them by his passions; while the good person, knowing his desires to be bad, is prevented from following them because of reason.
—Aristotle

The bad person, who strives only for pleasure, must be corrected by pain, like a beast of burden.
—Aristotle

The corrupt person is bad because he pursues an excess of bodily pleasure, not because he pursues any pleasure at all. For everyone enjoys good food, wine and sex, but not all do so in the right way.
—Aristotle

It is excess that makes pleasure harmful.
—Seneca

Self-imposed slavery is the most shameful of all.
—Seneca

People who have no self-restraint lead stormy and disordered lives.
—Seneca

*Control your cravings. Cut the strings of desire
which pull you around like a puppet.*
—Marcus Aurelius

No one is robbed of his own free will.
—Marcus Aurelius

*If we don't get what is desired, we continue to seek it and the mind is
still not satisfied. The only solution is to eliminate the selfish desire.*
—Zhu Xi

Do not drink or gamble without restraint.
—Zhu Xi

*Tis better to suppress the first desire than to satisfy all that follow
it. Tis easier to prevent bad habits than to break them.*
—Franklin

*Everything that frees our spirit without also
giving us self-control is ruinous.*
—Goethe

Avoid gambling. This is a vice which is productive of every possible evil.
—Washington

Would you be strong morally and physically? You must resist temptation.
—Churchill

Anger

When angry, the good man thinks about regret.
−Confucius

*The one who controls his anger, like a man controls a speeding chariot,
I call a charioteer. All others are just weakly holding the reins.*
−Buddha

Guard against anger in your speech.
−Buddha

*A good man should not lose his balance and not be carried away
by his emotions. He should only be angry for the right reasons,
in the proper amount, and for the correct length of time.*
−Aristotle

It doesn't matter how an insult is delivered, but how it is endured.
−Seneca

*Anger often comes to us, but more often we go to it. It should
never be invited and when it falls on us we should throw it off.*
−Seneca

*Our rage and grief do us more harm than whatever
caused our anger in the first place.*
−Marcus Aurelius

Anger is seldom without a reason, but seldom a good one.
−Franklin

Whatever is begun in anger ends in shame.
–Franklin

When a man gives way to anger he harms only himself.
–Gandhi

Animals

You do not become noble by injuring animals. By avoiding harm to animals one becomes noble.
–Buddha

Heaven, earth and the ten thousand creatures form one body with us.
–Zhu Xi

It is also vandalism wantonly to destroy or permit the destruction of what is beautiful in nature, whether it be a cliff, a forest, or a species of mammal or bird.
–Roosevelt

Any sport in which the death and torture of animals is made to furnish pleasure to the spectators is debasing.
–Roosevelt

Love the things that God has created, both animate and inanimate.
–Carver

The greatness of a nation can be judged by the way its animals are treated.
–Gandhi

Assertiveness

*To allow oneself to be insulted, or to look quietly on while
one's friends are being insulted, shows a slavish nature.*
–Aristotle

*First try to persuade others, but act against their
will when reason or justice demands it.*
–Marcus Aurelius

*If you have to respond to an attack, make your response
proportionate; but it is best if you can endure patiently.*
–Muhammad

*For a man to achieve all that is demanded of him, he
must consider himself more than he actually is.*
–Goethe

*Don't let anyone impose on you. Don't be quarrelsome, but stand up
for your rights. If you've got to fight, fight and fight hard and well.*
–Roosevelt

*A lady or gentleman takes his share of the world
and lets other people have theirs.*
–Carver

*A no uttered from deepest conviction is better than a yes
merely uttered to please, or worse, to avoid trouble.*
–Gandhi

They cannot take away our self-respect if we do not give it to them.
–Gandhi

Change

It is only the most wise and the most foolish who cannot change.
—Confucius

*Both the inability to change and the inability
to persevere are hostile to tranquility.*
—Seneca

The universe delights in change.
—Marcus Aurelius

*Truly accept that all things are subject to change, for there is
nothing like it to produce nobility and high-mindedness.*
—Marcus Aurelius

When you're finished changing, you're finished.
—Franklin

You must be the change you want to see in the world.
—Gandhi

*There is nothing wrong in change, if it is in the right direction. To
improve is to change, so to be perfect is to have changed often.*
—Churchill

Children

A good child is a gift from God.
—Ptah-Hotep

*Children strengthen the bonds between men and women, for children
are a shared good and what is shared holds people together.*
—Aristotle

When we educate our children we steer them by pleasure and pain.
—Aristotle

*Seize the pleasure your children bring and let them take joy
in you. Drink the cup of happiness dry without delay.*
—Seneca

It is only the parent who does not see talent in his child.
—Goethe

*For unflagging interest and enjoyment, a household of children,
if things go reasonably well, certainly makes all other forms of
success and achievement lose their importance by comparison.*
—Roosevelt

*No quality in a race atones for the failure to
produce an abundance of healthy children.*
—Roosevelt

*The inescapable duty of the good citizen of the right type
is to leave his or her blood behind in the world.*
—Roosevelt

It is easier to build a boy than to mend a man.
—Gandhi

There is no doubt that it is around the family and the home that all the greatest virtues, the most dominating virtues of human society, are created, strengthened, and maintained.
—Churchill

Citizenship and Community

Someone who provides nothing to the community receives no honor.
–Aristotle

When people do not look out for the common good it is ruined.
–Aristotle

*The good man does many things for the sake of his friends
and his country and will even die for them if he must.*
–Aristotle

If a house is divided against itself it cannot stand.
–Jesus

*There is nothing about which I am more anxious than my country,
and for its sake I am willing to die ten deaths if that be possible.*
–Elizabeth

Every post is honorable in which a man can serve his country.
–Washington

*When my country demands the sacrifice, personal ease
must always be a secondary consideration.*
–Washington

*The welfare of each of us is dependent fundamentally
upon the welfare of all of us.*
–Roosevelt

*There is no room in this country for hyphenated Americanism. The
one absolutely certain way of bringing this country to ruin, of
preventing all possibility of its continuing to be a nation at all, would
be to permit it to become a tangle of squabbling nationalities.*
—Roosevelt

*The good citizen is the man who, whatever his wealth
or his poverty, strives manfully to do his duty to himself,
to his family, to his neighbor, [and] to the state.*
—Roosevelt

Rights spring only from duties well done.
—Gandhi

*Seven social sins: politics without principles, wealth
without work, pleasure without conscience, knowledge
without character, commerce without morality, science
without humanity, and worship without sacrifice.*
—Gandhi

Conscience

*A divine spirit lives in us who watches our good and
bad deeds. He will treat us as we treat him.*
−Seneca

*I will do nothing based on what others think and everything
because of my conscience. Whatever I do when I am alone, I
will consider it done in front of all the people of Rome.*
−Seneca

A clear and innocent conscience fears nothing.
−Elizabeth

Would you live at ease, do what you ought, not as you please.
−Franklin

*Labor to keep alive in your breast that little
spark of celestial fire called conscience.*
−Washington

The only tyrant I will accept is the still, small voice within me.
−Gandhi

*There is a higher court than courts of justice
and that is the court of conscience.*
−Gandhi

Courage

A powerful and brave man who has no morals can cause great trouble.
—Confucius

*The brave person seems rash when compared to a coward,
but cowardly when compared to the foolhardy.*
—Aristotle

*We can become courageous by acting bravely in the
face of frightening things; and as we become truly
courageous, things become less frightening.*
—Aristotle

Brave people are eager when in action, but keep quiet beforehand.
—Aristotle

There are times when even to live is an act of bravery.
—Seneca

Great courage triumphs over great perils.
—Catherine

The coward only threatens when he is safe.
—Goethe

*No man is worth much anywhere if he does not
possess both moral and physical courage.*
—Roosevelt

*Alone of human beings, the good and wise mother stands
on a plane of equal honor with the bravest soldier.*
—Roosevelt

There were all kinds of things I was afraid of at first, ranging from grizzly bears to mean horses and gunfighters; but by acting as if I was not afraid I gradually ceased to be afraid.

–Roosevelt

It is easy to stand in a crowd but it takes courage to stand alone.

–Gandhi

Death

To seek death as a release from poverty or heartache or any other painful thing is not the act of a brave man, but of a coward.
—Aristotle

The day that you dread as your end is actually your birth into eternity.
—Seneca

A man will live ill if he does not know how to die well.
—Seneca

Living is not enough, but to live well. The wise man will go on living as long as he should, not just as long as he likes.
—Seneca

Even dying is an act of life, and as with everything else, you should do your best.
—Marcus Aurelius

Every part of me will be transformed into another part of the universe, and that will again be changed into another, and so on forever.
—Marcus Aurelius

You boarded the ship, you have sailed, and you have reached port. Now get off! If it is the start of a new life, you will find the Gods there too. If it is the end of all, you will be liberated from the tyranny of pleasure and pain.
—Marcus Aurelius

I want to be allowed to die at my ease, and in peace.
—Elizabeth

Fear not death; for the sooner we die the longer we shall be immortal.
—Franklin

The dead being dead, we must think of the living.
—Catherine

When the summons comes, I shall endeavor to obey it with good grace.
—Washington

I die hard, but I am not afraid to go. Tis well.
—Washington's last words

I am convinced that our spirit is indestructible and that its activity continues for all eternity. It is like the sun, which seems to set before our earthly eyes but in reality shines unceasingly.
—Goethe

Both life and death are part of the same great adventure.
—Roosevelt

To appreciate that the great mystery shall not be known to us, and so living, to face the beyond confident and without fear—that is life.
—Roosevelt

After I leave this world, I do not believe I am through.
—Carver

We have no evidence whatsoever that the soul perishes with the body.
—Gandhi

Noble spirits yield themselves willingly to the successively falling shades which carry them to a better world or to oblivion.
—Churchill

Drunkenness

*Those who kill, lie, steal, seduce another's wife, and
drink to excess are digging their own graves.*
—Buddha

*Drunkenness inflames and lays bare every vice, removing
the self-control that checks bad behavior.*
—Seneca

*They ask you about wine and gambling—in both there is great sin
and some benefit to people, but the sin is greater than the benefit.*
—Muhammad

Drinking does not drown care, but waters it, and makes it grow faster.
—Franklin

*Drunkenness, that worst of evils, makes some
mere fools, some beasts, and some devils.*
—Franklin

Early Rising

The wise will wake up early to their gain, while the ignorant fall behind.
—Ptah-Hotep

*It is a disgrace if someone lies in bed, half-
asleep when the sun is high in the sky.*
—Seneca

Up sluggard and waste not life; in the grave will be sleeping enough.
—Franklin

Early to bed and early to rise, makes a man healthy, wealthy, and wise.
—Franklin

Equality and Fair Play

*While the gentleman cherishes fairness, the small
man cherishes special treatment.*

—Confucius

*Who can state that nature has been ungenerous to women's natures
and has narrowly restricted their virtues? Believe me, they have just
as much energy and aptitude for noble actions; they are just as able to
endure suffering and toil when they have grown accustomed to it.*

—Seneca

*The equality of citizens consists in that they
should all be subject to the same laws.*

—Catherine

*We must treat each man on his worth and merits as a man.
We must see that each is given a square deal because he
is entitled to no more and should receive no less.*

—Roosevelt

There can be no question that women should have equal rights with men.

—Roosevelt

*Women should have free access to every field of labor
which they care to enter, and when their work is as
valuable as that of a man it should be paid as highly.*

—Roosevelt

*We are all brothers, all of us, no matter what race or color
or condition. We rise together or we fall together.*

—Carver

*I am trying to get our people to see that their color
does not hold them back as much as they think.*
—Carver

*Rising or falling I believe is practically inherent within the
individual, and since races are made up of individuals,
they progress or are held back by the percentage of
individuals who will or will not do the right thing.*
—Carver

*When I think of what women did in the war, I feel
sure they deserve to be treated equally.*
—Churchill

To call woman the weaker sex is libel.
—Gandhi

Forgiveness

How much better it is to heal a wrong than to avenge one.
−Seneca

Forgive and you will be forgiven.
−Jesus

A person who is patient and forgives is surely following the divine path.
−Muhammad

*Cast off your hurt feelings and resentment
and you get rid of the wrong itself.*
−Marcus Aurelius

It is better to take many injuries than to give one.
−Franklin

The weak can never forgive. Forgiveness is an attribute of the strong.
−Gandhi

An eye for an eye will only make the whole world blind.
−Gandhi

We must abandon all bitterness and all wish for revenge.
−Churchill

Friends

*If you find a companion who is wise and good, you should
travel together in enjoyment, overcoming all dangers.*

−Buddha

*Keeping company with fools is like going on
a long journey with an enemy.*

−Buddha

Friendship is not only necessary for us but noble.

−Aristotle

*The mere presence of friends is sweet in times of good or bad fortune;
for even our pain is lightened when friends share it with us.*

−Aristotle

Nothing can equal the pleasure of loving and loyal friendship.

−Seneca

*After a friendship is formed you must trust,
but before that you must judge.*

−Seneca

Greater love has no one than this: to lay down one's life for one's friend.

−Jesus

The noble person must exalt his teachers and feel affection for his friends.

−Zhu Xi

Prosperity provideth but adversity proveth friends.

−Elizabeth

I am a friend not won with trifles, nor lost with the like.
—Elizabeth

Friendship is the uniform consent of two minds, such as
virtue links and naught but death can destroy.
—Elizabeth

A true friend is the best possession.
—Franklin

It is only in life's most demanding situations that
one can distinguish true from false friends.
—Catherine

Be courteous to all but intimate with few, and let those few
be well tried before you give them your confidence.
—Washington

Associate yourself with men of good quality if you esteem your
own reputation; for tis better to be alone than in bad company.
—Washington

Tell me who you associate with and I will tell you who you are.
—Goethe

It is much easier to join bad companions than to shake them off.
—Churchill

Giving and Charity

Share what you have with your friends; you have it by the grace of God.
—Ptah-Hotep

The good person helps out the needy; he does
not make the rich even richer.
—Confucius

Misers do not go to live with the Gods because they will not give, but
the wise love generosity and so find happiness in the next world.
—Buddha

Gifts to the community are like offerings to the Gods.
—Aristotle

There is no pleasure in possessing something of value
unless you have someone to share it with.
—Seneca

Give and it will be given to you.
—Jesus

If I have acted charitably then I have benefited by it.
—Marcus Aurelius

Do not forget to be generous to each other.
—Muhammad

Share with one another and sympathize with one another in difficulties.
—Zhu Xi

Do good to do good, that's all.
—Catherine

Let your heart feel the affliction and distress of everyone;
let your hand give in proportion to your purse.
—Washington

Generosity wins favor with everyone,
especially when it is done modestly.
—Goethe

Remember that every man at times stumbles and must be helped up; if
he lies down, you cannot carry him. He has got to be willing to walk.
—Roosevelt

Shame on him who will not stretch out a helping hand to his brother.
—Roosevelt

It is not the style of clothes one wears, neither the kind of automobile
one drives, nor the amount of money one has in the bank that counts.
These mean nothing. It is simply service that measures success.
—Carver

The best way to find yourself is to lose yourself in the service of others.
—Gandhi

Goals

*Fools imagine trivial things to be vital for life and
never attain great knowledge or happiness.*
—Buddha

*Leave alone what cannot be or is unlikely to be attained, focus
on what is near at hand and is within hope of reach.*
—Seneca

*Put your hand to projects you can finish or at least
hope to finish; avoid projects that expand as you work
on them or do not stop at the place you intend.*
—Seneca

*Let good heed be taken lest in reaching too far after
future good, you peril not the present.*
—Elizabeth

A just cause is the first step on the way to glory.
—Catherine

*In thought as well as in action, we must distinguish
between what is and is not attainable. Without this little
can be achieved, either in life or in knowledge.*
—Goethe

Beware of scattering your efforts, instead try to concentrate them.
—Goethe

*Practical efficiency is common, and lofty idealism is not uncommon;
it is the combination that is necessary and the combination is rare.*
—Roosevelt

When we undertake the impossible, we often fail to do anything at all.
—Roosevelt

Nourish your hopes, but do not overlook realities.
—Churchill

*Perfect solutions to our difficulties are not to
be looked for in an imperfect world.*
—Churchill

Golden Rule

Never do to others what you do not want done to you.
—Confucius

All creatures love life. All creatures fear pain.
Therefore treat all creatures as yourself.
—Buddha

Treat the weak as you would like the strong to treat you.
—Seneca

Do to others as you would have them do to you.
—Jesus

A gentleman scorns equally to wrong others
or to suffer others to wrong him.
—Roosevelt

Gossip

Do not repeat slanderous rumors, don't even listen to them.
Gossip is the common language of the angry and overexcited.
Only report on a thing you have observed, not just heard.
—Ptah-Hotep

Do not malign anyone great or small, the spirit abhors it.
—Ptah-Hotep

If you listen carefully, set aside what you are unsure of and
speak cautiously of the rest, you will make few mistakes.
—Confucius

Those who repeat gossip are without virtue.
—Confucius

The man who tries to find out what has been said against him,
who tries to unearth spiteful gossip, even when spoken privately,
is responsible for destroying his own peace of mind.
—Seneca

Do not speak ill of one another.
—Muhammad

It is the custom of evil mouths to say the worse, rather than the better.
—Elizabeth

Hear no ill of a friend, nor speak any of an enemy.
—Franklin

To speak evil of anyone, unless there is unequivocal proof of their
deserving it, is an injury for which there is no adequate reparation.
—Washington

Government and Politics

Men are more wicked together than separately.
—Seneca

There is nothing more to say about governance as long as the ruler is respectful, moderate, and fond of goodness.
—Zhu Xi

Those who would give up essential liberty to purchase a little temporary safety deserve neither liberty nor safety.
—Franklin

Commerce flies from places where it meets oppression and settles where it has protection.
—Catherine

When a people become incapable of governing themselves and fit for a master, it is of little consequence from what quarter he comes.
—Washington

Let me warn you in the most solemn manner against the baneful effects of the spirit of party. It serves always to distract the public councils and enfeebles the public administration.
—Washington

Which is the best form of government? That which teaches us to govern ourselves.
—Goethe

Deep and serious thinkers are generally on bad terms with the public.
—Goethe

Order without liberty and liberty without order are equally destructive.
—Roosevelt

*People show themselves unfit for liberty when they
submit to either anarchy or tyranny.*
—Roosevelt

*In popular government results worth having can be achieved only
by men who combine worthy ideals with practical good sense.*
—Roosevelt

A vote is like a rifle: its usefulness depends upon the character of the user.
—Roosevelt

Democracy disciplined and enlightened is the finest thing in the world.
—Gandhi

*No one pretends that Democracy is perfect or all-wise. Indeed it has
been said that Democracy is the worst form of government except
all those other forms that have been tried from time to time.*
—Churchill

*Some people's idea of free speech is that they are free to say what
they like, but if anyone else says something back, that is an outrage.*
—Churchill

*The alteration of Parties in power, like the
rotation of crops, has beneficial results.*
—Churchill

Gratitude

Most people are forgetful of favors done for them and seek to receive more benefits than they give.

—Aristotle

Be silent about the favors you have done, but speak openly of the favors you have received.

—Seneca

You ask what is your greatest fault? Your accounting is wrong: you rate too high the value of what you have given and too low what you have received.

—Seneca

The true sin against God is ingratitude.

—Elizabeth

Most people return small favors, acknowledge middling ones, and repay great ones with ingratitude.

—Franklin

Ingratitude is always a kind of weakness. I have never known men of ability to be ungrateful.

—Goethe

Happiness

Let your face be bright and cheerful as long as you live.
—Ptah-Hotep

The happy person lives well and acts well.
—Aristotle

Let us be cheerful and brave whatever befalls us.
—Seneca

Nature's intention was that we should need very little to live in happiness; every one of us is capable of making ourselves happy.
—Seneca

Angry looks offend against nature. An unhappy face causes beauty to fade away.
—Marcus Aurelius

Happiness and misery depend upon ourselves. If you feel sadness, rise above it and act so that your happiness does not depend upon any outside event.
—Catherine

One must be cheerful. That is the only way to overcome and endure everything.
—Catherine

Happiness depends more upon the internal frame of a person's mind than on the externals of the world.
—Washington

See the good in all things.
—Carver

*Happiness is when what you think, what you
say, and what you do are in harmony.*
—Gandhi

True happiness does not come from without, it comes only from within.
—Gandhi

*For myself I am an optimist—it does not seem
to be much use being anything else.*
—Churchill

Hardship

*A good man can withstand hardship, while
a small man is swept away by it.*
—Confucius

*A wise man will bear with dignity whatever fortune sends and
will always make the best of his circumstances, just as a good
general makes the best use of the forces he has on hand.*
—Aristotle

It matters not what you bear but how you bear it.
—Seneca

*Good fortune can come to small men and to men of inferior talents, but
to triumph over disasters and terrors is the privilege of the great man.*
—Seneca

*No one is less fortunate than the man who has never met
adversity, for he has never had the pleasure of testing himself.*
—Seneca

Disaster is virtue's opportunity.
—Seneca

Bad luck borne nobly is good luck.
—Marcus Aurelius

No gains without pains.
—Franklin

Be not disturbed by trifles, or at accidents common or unavoidable.
—Franklin

Only in misfortune can a resilient spirit be seen.
—Catherine

It is our duty to make the best of our misfortunes.
—Washington

We ought not to convert trifling difficulties into insuperable obstacles.
—Washington

We should not wish adversity on anyone, but to face hardship by chance builds character and is of the most decisive value to men.
—Goethe

Difficulties increase the nearer we get to the goal.
—Goethe

After all, the saddest thing that can happen to a man is to carry no burdens.
—Roosevelt

It is a man's privilege to overcome adverse circumstances.
—Gandhi

Difficulties mastered are opportunities won.
—Churchill

A pessimist sees the difficulty in every opportunity. An optimist sees the opportunity in every difficulty.
—Churchill

Health

Health is the best possession, contentment the greatest wealth.
—Buddha

Health is man's best wealth.
—Franklin

*Unless you avoid extremes you will undermine
your health for no good reason.*
—Catherine

It is health that is the real wealth and not pieces of gold and silver.
—Gandhi

Heroes

The superior man stands in awe of three things: the decrees
of heaven, great men, and the words of the sages.
–Confucius

Think about the benefit that good example provides us, and you will
realize that great men's presence and their memory are both useful.
–Seneca

Have before you at all times the image of a
great man who practiced virtue.
–Marcus Aurelius

Heroes are so rare. I should wish to see them all assembled in paradise.
–Catherine

Let us take council of the past, and draw wisdom and courage
from the memory of great men who have gone before us.
–Churchill

Honesty

The wise man will not let a penny that would enter dishonestly into his house.
–Seneca

It is shameful to say one thing and do another.
–Seneca

Whoever is dishonest with very little things will also be dishonest with much.
–Jesus

Give weight and measure with fairness; do not cheat anyone out of what is rightly theirs.
–Muhammad

If a person is not true to himself or true to his word, then all of his affairs will be without foundation.
–Zhu Xi

What you would seem to be, be really.
–Franklin

Half a truth is often a great lie.
–Franklin

Intrigues are the means of the weak.
–Catherine

Nothing should be more strictly forbidden and more harshly treated than lying.
–Catherine

167

Honesty is always the best policy.
−Washington

If anyone lies, if he has the habit of untruthfulness, you cannot deal with him, because there is nothing to depend on.
−Roosevelt

A lady or gentleman is too generous to cheat.
−Carver

To believe in something and not to live it is dishonest.
−Gandhi

Humor

Those who jest gracefully are called witty. But the buffoon cannot resist causing laughter, sparing neither himself nor others and saying things that no refined man would say. Lastly the boor is useless with regards to humor for he contributes nothing and takes everything badly.
—Aristotle

It is better to laugh at life than to cry over it.
—Seneca

He who laughs last, laughs best.
—Catherine

Nothing shows a man's character more than by what he laughs at.
—Goethe

If I had no sense of humor, I should long ago have committed suicide.
—Gandhi

Industry and Hard Work

Don't waste a moment, for missed opportunities
will be regretted when your life is over.
—Buddha

It is not manly to be afraid of sweat.
—Seneca

Does not any industrious man find idleness a punishment?
—Seneca

Those who are diligent and swift in their work will
acquire more; those who do not make an effort and
are slow will acquire less; it is a natural law.
—Zhu Xi

God helps them that help themselves.
—Franklin

Diligence is the mother of good luck.
—Franklin

Nothing should be more highly prized than the value of each day.
—Goethe

There has never yet been a man in our history who led
a life of ease whose name is worth remembering.
—Roosevelt

We cannot do great deeds unless we are willing to do the
small things that make up the sum of greatness.
—Roosevelt

A small body of determined spirits fired by an unquenchable
faith in their mission can alter the course of history.
–Gandhi

The difference between what we do and what we are capable of
doing would suffice to solve most of the world's problems.
–Gandhi

No one should waste a day.
–Churchill

How little we should worry about anything other than doing our best.
–Churchill

Judging

When you meet someone better than yourself, strive to become his equal. When you meet a bad man, look within and examine yourself.

—Confucius

Do not focus on the faults of others or what they have or haven't done. Instead think about what you have and have not done.

—Buddha

You stare at other men's blemishes when you yourself are covered in open sores.

—Seneca

Why do you look at the speck of sawdust in your brother's eye and pay no attention to the plank in your own eye?

—Jesus

Do not judge and you will not be judged.

—Jesus

Remember the best measure of a man is the worth of the things he cares about.

—Marcus Aurelius

Do not look around at the bad behavior of others, look ahead and run straight toward your goal.

—Marcus Aurelius

Do not be hasty in your judgments.

—Catherine

To judge a man well, one must put oneself in his place.
—Catherine

I shall never attempt to palliate my own
faults by exposing those of others.
—Washington

There are people who focus on the defects of their friends, but
there is nothing to be gained by it. I have always paid attention
to the merits of my opponents and found it very rewarding.
—Goethe

Whenever I see an erring man, I say to myself I have also erred.
—Gandhi

Justice and Mercy

Evil may prosper in the short term, but in the end justice will prevail.
−Ptah-Hotep

*Punish evil firmly and correct wrongs strongly to eliminate
vice and maintain virtue. But make sure the punishment
fits the crime or you become the wrongdoer.*
−Ptah-Hotep

Repay injustice with justice. Repay kindness with kindness.
−Confucius

Justice is the sum of all virtues.
−Aristotle

You can become just by doing just actions.
−Aristotle

*When vengeance is easy, the man who refuses
it wins unqualified praise for mercy.*
−Seneca

Blessed are the merciful, for they will be shown mercy.
−Jesus

Injustice can result as often from doing nothing as from doing something.
−Marcus Aurelius

All other virtues are rooted in justice.
−Marcus Aurelius

God loves the just.
—Muhammad

Justice, truth, and reason are an invulnerable shield.
—Catherine

Nothing in the world can hide unjust actions.
—Catherine

It is better to prevent crimes than to punish them.
—Catherine

A great deal may be done by harshness; even more by love;
but most by clear judgment and impartial justice.
—Goethe

Treat each man whatever his color, his creed, or his social
position with evenhanded justice on his real merits as a man.
—Roosevelt

One ought to be just before one is generous.
—Churchill

The finest combination in the world is power and mercy.
—Churchill

Kindness

It is a man's kindly acts that are remembered after he is gone.
—Ptah-Hotep

Just as your family and friends greet you with joy after a long journey, so will your good deeds joyfully await you in the next life.
—Buddha

Those who seek happiness by causing pain to others are caught in a net of hatred from which they cannot escape.
—Buddha

Wherever there is a human being there is an opportunity for an act of kindness.
—Seneca

One thing alone can bring us peace, to agree to treat each other with kindness.
—Seneca

He who does a good deed will be repaid tenfold.
—Muhammad

When one is without self-centered desires, kindness begins to appear, just as when there are no obstructions blocking the way, water begins to flow.
—Zhu Xi

It is seldom that we get to satisfy ourselves; so it is all the more rewarding when we can satisfy others.
—Goethe

The simplest acts of kindness are by far more powerful than a thousand heads bowing in prayer.
—Gandhi

Know Yourself

Vain men are fools as well as ignorant of themselves
and make this clear to everyone.
−Aristotle

It is critical that a man reach a true estimate of himself,
for we generally overestimate our abilities.
−Seneca

Failing to understand the workings of your own
mind is sure to lead to unhappiness.
−Marcus Aurelius

If we examine ourselves, we will be clear and will master the darkness.
−Zhu Xi

They are most deceived that trusteth most in themselves.
−Elizabeth

Observe all men, thyself most.
−Franklin

We ought not to deceive ourselves.
−Washington

It is a great error to see yourself as more or less than you truly are.
−Goethe

The man who can admit to his limitations is the closest to perfection.
−Goethe

It is good to see ourselves as others see us.
    –Gandhi

A man learns more from his critics than his followers.
    –Gandhi

Leadership

If you are powerful, act in a way that wins you respect for your wisdom and moderation. Make farsighted decisions and don't simply react to events.
—Ptah-Hotep

Raise up the straight and set them over the crooked. This can make the crooked straight.
—Confucius

Good men are easy to serve but difficult to please.
—Confucius

The common people can be made to follow a path but not to understand it.
—Confucius

The tyrant only considers his own advantage, but the king considers the advantage of his subjects.
—Aristotle

Value men not by their jobs, but by their character.
—Seneca

Have them respect rather than fear you.
—Seneca

It is best to establish regulations that are simple and easy so that people can follow them.
—Zhu Xi

One man with a head on his shoulders is worth a dozen without.
−Elizabeth

It is infinitely better to have a few good men than many indifferent ones.
−Washington

*Make the best of mankind as they are since
we cannot have them as we wish.*
−Washington

It is easy to know how to rule but hard to know how to govern well.
−Goethe

Love engenders love, and one who is loved can easily govern.
−Goethe

*The man in command must take all the risks which he asks his
men to take if he is going to get the best work out of them.*
−Roosevelt

He who wants to please all will please none.
−Gandhi

A leader is the greatest servant.
−Gandhi

A man of character will make himself worthy of any position he is given.
−Gandhi

Where there is great power there is great responsibility.
−Churchill

Leading by Example

A good man puts his actions before his words.
—Confucius

Like a beautiful flower, full of color but lacking fragrance, so are the words of those who do not practice what they preach.
—Buddha

Men can prove that their words are their own; let them practice what they preach.
—Seneca

It is hateful to God that you say things and then do not practice them.
—Muhammad

Well done is better than well said.
—Franklin

A good example is the best sermon.
—Franklin

Example is the most potent of all things.
—Roosevelt

The man who preaches decency and straight dealing occupies a particularly contemptible position if he does not try himself to practice what he preaches.
—Roosevelt

An ounce of practice is worth more than tons of preaching.
—Gandhi

Life

*To be neither modest nor respectful when young, to
accomplish nothing worth passing on when grown, and
to refuse to die when old—that is what I call a pest.*

−Confucius

*People forget their lives will end soon. For
those who remember, quarrels end.*

−Buddha

*Better to live in virtue and wisdom for one day than to live one hundred
years ill-behaved and undisciplined. Better to live with insight and
wisdom for one day than to live one hundred years unwise. Better to live
one day with vigor and effort than one hundred years idle and lazy.*

−Buddha

The life we are given is not short, but we make it so.

−Seneca

*As with a play so it is with life. What matters is not how
long it is, but how well it has been performed.*

−Seneca

A long life may not be good enough, but a good life is long enough.

−Franklin

If thou would live long, live well; for folly and wickedness shorten life.

−Franklin

*How far you go in life depends on your being tender with the young,
compassionate with the aged, sympathetic with the striving, and tolerant of
the weak and strong. Because someday in your life you will be all of these.*

−Washington

The worst of all fears is the fear of living.
—Roosevelt

Life is a great adventure ... accept it in such a spirit.
—Roosevelt

*No individual has any right to come into this world
and go out of it without leaving behind him distinct and
legitimate reasons for having passed through it.*
—Carver

*One of the things that has helped me as much as any other is not
how long I am going to live but how much I can do while living.*
—Carver

Live simply so others may simply live.
—Gandhi

Live as if you were to die tomorrow; learn as if you were to live forever.
—Gandhi

*What is the use of living, if it be not to strive for noble
causes and make this muddled world a better place
for those who will live in it after we are gone?*
—Churchill

*Live dangerously; take things as they come;
dread naught, all will be well.*
—Churchill

Love

As ill will increases strife, so goodwill increases love.
—Ptah-Hotep

Love your fellow man.
—Confucius

Hatred does not end by hatred, but by love.
—Buddha

Friendship lies more in loving than being loved.
—Aristotle

If you want to be loved, then love.
—Seneca

Love your neighbor as yourself.
—Jesus

Love mankind; walk with God.
—Marcus Aurelius

Love the people in your life without reservation.
—Marcus Aurelius

Be loving in dealing with all things.
—Zhu Xi

In the face of another's excellence the only possible salvation is love.
—Goethe

Where there is love there is God also.
—Gandhi

Manners

Manners are a matter of being respectful.
−Zhu Xi

Be civil to all; sociable to many; familiar with few.
−Franklin

Women's company is the basis of good manners.
−Goethe

Courtesy is as much the mark of a gentleman as courage.
−Roosevelt

A lady or gentleman is always considerate of women, children, and old people.
−Carver

We lose nothing by using common courtesy.
−Gandhi

Marriage

*If you wish to be wise, look after your family and love
your wife with passion. Fill her stomach, clothe her
back and gladden her heart as long as you live.*
—Ptah-Hotep

*Four things happen to the man who goes with another's wife:
shame, sleepless nights, condemnation and increased suffering.*
—Buddha

*Men and women share a household not only to have children, but also
to enhance their lives. The skills of men and women are clearly different
and each contributes to the others needs in service of their common good.*
—Aristotle

*No one can lead a happy life if he thinks only of himself
and tries to turn everything to his own advantage. You must
live for someone else if you wish to live for yourself.*
—Seneca

Therefore what God has joined together, let no one separate.
—Jesus

*God created mates for you to live with in tranquility; and
he has ordained love and kindness between you.*
—Muhammad

Have nothing to do with adultery, it is a foul thing and an evil path.
—Muhammad

*The marriage of husbands and wives is the
beginning of human relationships.*
—Zhu Xi

*The flourishing of good fortune is always based in the household;
the decline of the Way always starts in the home.*
—Zhu Xi

*I do not want a husband who honors me as a
queen, if he does not love me as a woman.*
—Elizabeth

He that has not got a wife, is not yet a complete man.
—Franklin

*Marriage is the proper remedy. It is the most natural state of man, and
therefore the state in which you are most likely to find solid happiness.*
—Franklin

Married in haste, we oft repent at leisure.
—Franklin

*I have always considered marriage as the most interesting
event in one's life, the foundation of happiness or misery.*
—Washington

*No words can paint the scorn and contempt which must be felt by all
right-thinking men, not only for the brutal husband, but the husband
who fails to show full loyalty and consideration to his wife.*
—Roosevelt

A man must think well before he marries.
—Roosevelt

*If the husband is a god, the wife is also a goddess.
She is not a slave, but a friend and companion with
equal rights. Each is the teacher of the other.*
—Gandhi

Mistakes

When you have made a mistake, do not be afraid of correcting yourself.
—Confucius

When a small man makes a mistake, he is sure to hide it.
—Confucius

A man who does not know he is blundering sees no need to change:
you must catch yourself at fault before you can correct yourself.
—Seneca

When someone makes a mistake correct him gently and
show him his error. When you make a mistake, blame
only yourself, or even better, blame no one.
—Marcus Aurelius

Remember that to accept correction and change your mind
when someone points out a mistake allows more freedom
than feeling obligated to persist in your error.
—Marcus Aurelius

If there are errors, one ought to change quickly;
do not, fearing difficulty, blindly persist.
—Zhu Xi

He who does his best is not held to do more.
—Elizabeth

None but the well-bred man knows how to confess
a fault or acknowledge himself in error.
—Franklin

We shouldn't be afraid to give way when we are rightly contradicted.
—Goethe

A strong and wise people will study its failures no less than its triumphs, for there is wisdom to be learned from the study of both.
—Roosevelt

Confession of errors is like a broom which sweeps away the dirt and leaves the surface brighter and cleaner.
—Gandhi

Moderation

To exceed is as bad as to fall short.
—Confucius

Supreme indeed is the middle path.
—Confucius

*Avoiding extremes, the middle way produces insight and
wisdom, leading to tranquility and enlightenment.*
—Buddha

A master in any art avoids what is too much or too little.
—Aristotle

*Excess and deficiency are related to vice, moderation to virtue—for
we are good in only one way, but bad in many different ways.*
—Aristotle

Anything carried to excess is wrong.
—Seneca

To practice the mean is the true way of the Universe.
—Zhu Xi

*Reaching the mean, one is sometimes dignified and resolute, sometimes
compassionate and compliant, but always moderately regulated
and lacking the imbalance of going too far or not far enough.*
—Zhu Xi

*To overshoot or to fall short fails to maintain balance. Practicing
the mean and keeping constant alone constitutes perfection.*
—Zhu Xi

Avoid extremes.
 —Franklin

Extremes should always be avoided.
 —Gandhi

Modesty

Do not exalt yourself and you will not be humbled.
−Ptah-Hotep

Do not be arrogant because of what you know;
consult with both the ignorant and the wise.
−Ptah-Hotep

The good man is dignified without being arrogant.
The small man is arrogant without dignity.
−Confucius

A good man is ashamed to let his words outstrip his deeds.
−Confucius

An attempt to look impressive around those less fortunate
is as bad as a strong man picking on a cripple.
−Aristotle

Be careful not to practice your righteousness in
front of others to be seen by them.
−Jesus

Be modest in success and graceful in failure.
−Marcus Aurelius

God does not like arrogant or boastful people.
−Muhammad

To be humble to superiors is duty, to equals
courtesy, to inferiors nobleness.
−Franklin

He that falls in love with himself will have no rivals.
—Franklin

People who are wrapped up in themselves make small packages.
—Franklin

The emptiest people think very highly of themselves; the best are mistrustful.
—Goethe

A lady or gentleman loses, if needs be, without squealing; and wins without bragging.
—Carver

Nature

Every part of nature has its marvels.
—Aristotle

If we follow nature everything will be easy and straightforward,
but if we struggle against it, life is just like rowing upstream.
—Seneca

Remember God's blessings and do not lay the Earth to waste.
—Muhammad

A person of true goodness regards heaven, earth,
and the myriad things as one body.
—Zhu Xi

Nature hides God—but not from everyone.
—Goethe

Nature does not joke, she is always true, always serious, and
always right; the errors and faults are always those of man.
—Goethe

The fresh air of the open country is our proper
element; it is like the breath of God.
—Goethe

Wild flowers should be enjoyed unplucked where they grow.
—Roosevelt

The further one gets into the wilderness, the greater
is the attraction of its lonely freedom.
—Roosevelt

To waste, to destroy our natural resources, to skin and exhaust the land instead of using it so as to increase its usefulness, will result in undermining in the days of our children the very prosperity which we ought by right to hand down to them amplified and developed.
—Roosevelt

Leave it as it is. You cannot improve on it. The ages have been at work on it, and man can only mar it.
—Roosevelt

Talk to nature and let nature talk to you.
—Carver

Nature will drive away those who commit sins against it.
—Carver

Whenever the soil is rich the people flourish, physically and economically. Whenever the soil is wasted the people are wasted.
—Carver

You can't tear up everything to get the dollar out without suffering as a result.
—Carver

The good man is a friend to all living things.
—Gandhi

I need no inspiration other than nature.
—Gandhi

No one should ever cut one down without planting another. It is much easier to cut trees than to grow them.
—Churchill

Old Age

Gray hair does not make one an elder. One can grow old and just become an old fool.

−Buddha

A man who does not learn from life grows old like an ox. His body grows but not his mind.

−Buddha

The ravages of time are easier to see in others.

−Seneca

Life's tragedy is that we get old too soon and wise too late.

−Franklin

It does not become an old man to run after fashion, either in thought or dress.

−Goethe

Age merely shows what children we remain.

−Goethe

Overeating and Gluttony

The good man does not go on eating until he is full.
—Confucius

*It is difficult for a man who always has a full stomach
to put his heart and mind to some use.*
—Confucius

*Eating too much and sleeping too much, like an overfed pig
the foolish man gets what he deserves in the next life.*
—Buddha

You should not eat until hunger commands you.
—Seneca

*Would you count someone as a human being whose highest
good consists of flavors and colors and sounds? He should
be crossed off the list of our species. An animal whose
delight is fodder should herd instead with cattle.*
—Seneca

Eat to live; live not to eat.
—Franklin

We should then eat to live, not live to eat.
—Gandhi

Passions

Passion seems to yield to force but not to reason.
–Aristotle

It is easier to exclude harmful passions than to control them.
–Seneca

If passion drives let reason hold the reins.
–Franklin

Great passions are hopeless diseases.
–Goethe

If there is one quality which is not admirable, whether in a nation or in an individual, it is hysterics, either in religion or in anything else.
–Roosevelt

Patience

Do not be impatient and do not get distracted by small opportunities. If you try to rush things, you will not reach your goal. If you only focus on small opportunities, you will not accomplish more important things.
—Confucius

I will endure harsh words patiently, just as the elephant endures arrows on the battlefield.
—Buddha

Haste makes waste.
—Franklin

What is postponed is not lost.
—Catherine

Everything is possible with patience and effort.
—Gandhi

Patience, however, and good temper accomplish much.
—Churchill

Perseverance

*It is shameful for the spirit to surrender when the
body is willing to continue the struggle.*
—Marcus Aurelius

God is with those who are resolute.
—Muhammad

The essential thing is not to give up. If you give up, you will not succeed.
—Zhu Xi

You will find me a rock that bends to no wind.
—Elizabeth

Energy and persistence conquer all things.
—Franklin

Perseverance and spirit have done wonders in all ages.
—Washington

*There is no situation that cannot be ennobled
by hard work or by endurance.*
—Goethe

*All daring and courage, all iron endurance of misfortune
make for a finer and nobler type of manhood.*
—Roosevelt

*Ninety-nine percent of the failures come from people
who have the habit of making excuses.*
—Carver

Never give in! Never give in! Never, never, never, never—
in nothing great or small, large or petty—never give in
except to convictions of honor and good sense.
—Churchill

We must be equally good at what is short and
sharp and what is long and tough.
—Churchill

Planning

*He who does not worry about distant troubles will soon
have something worse than worry close at hand.*
−Confucius

If you ignore the details, great plans will come to nothing.
−Confucius

A good beginning is more than half the race.
−Aristotle

It is in times of security that the mind should be prepared for hardship.
−Seneca

*The man who anticipates the coming of troubles
takes away their power when they arrive.*
−Seneca

*If you do not see where to begin, it doesn't matter whether
you proceed quickly or slowly—you will not succeed.*
−Zhu Xi

Haste often spoils the best plans.
−Elizabeth

A fool too late bewares when all peril is past.
−Elizabeth

The most simple plans are often the best, and the most complex the worst.
−Catherine

Fortune is not as blind as people think. It is often the result of a long series of precise and well-chosen steps that precede the events and that are not perceived by the common herd.
—Catherine

He who looks ahead is lord of the day.
—Goethe

When a man asks for too much and delights in complexity, he is asking for trouble.
—Goethe

The greatest difficulties are located where we are not expecting them.
—Goethe

There is no shortcut to achievement. Life requires thorough preparation—veneer isn't worth anything.
—Carver

When danger is far off we may think of our weakness; when it is near we must not forget our strength.
—Churchill

Popularity and Fame

The superior man is troubled by his lack of ability,
not by the failure of others to appreciate him.
—Confucius

As a solid rock cannot be moved by the wind, the
wise are not moved by praise or blame.
—Buddha

If you do not respect yourself, you make your
happiness subject to the opinions of others.
—Marcus Aurelius

I will not seek or retain popularity at the expense
of one social duty or moral virtue.
—Washington

Sometimes it is not wise to look for too much appreciation. The
main thing is to make sure you are right and go ahead regardless
of whether people appreciate it or whether they don't.
—Carver

I always prefer to accept the guidance of my heart
to the calculations of public feeling.
—Churchill

Possessions

Sorrow cannot attack those who never try to possess people and things as their own.
—Buddha

How happily we live; we who own nothing.
—Buddha

Never judge a man by what he has but by who he is.
—Seneca

A man is a fool if he only looks at the saddle and bridle when he goes to buy a horse; but he is a greater fool if he judges a man only by his clothes and position.
—Seneca

We don't realize how unnecessary many things are until they begin to run out.
—Seneca

Life does not consist in an abundance of possessions.
—Jesus

Don't focus so much on the things you do not have.
—Marcus Aurelius

Do not conceive that fine clothes make fine men, any more than fine feathers make fine birds.
—Washington

It is sinful to multiply one's wants unnecessarily.
—Gandhi

Practice

We become good builders by building and good harpers by harping. Similarly we become just by doing just actions, moderate by doing moderate actions, and brave by doing brave actions.

–Aristotle

What you begin out of necessity can gradually become a pleasure.

–Seneca

Also practice the things which you don't expect to master.

–Marcus Aurelius

Not only what he is born with, but also what he acquires makes the man.

–Goethe

Procrastination

*The greatest waste in life comes from procrastination.
It takes from us each day as it comes, robbing the
present from us based on promises of the future.*
—Seneca

Everything in the future is uncertain: Live here and now!
—Seneca

*What is close is difficult; what is distant is easy—but if you do
not do the difficult first, you will never be able to do the easy.*
—Zhu Xi

Lost time is never found again.
—Franklin

*Dost thou love life? Then do not squander time;
for that is the stuff life is made of.*
—Franklin

But what is your duty? What the day demands.
—Goethe

*There are two days in the year that we cannot
do anything, yesterday and tomorrow.*
—Gandhi

*The era of procrastination, of half measures, of soothing
and baffling expedients, of delays, is coming to an end. In
its place we are entering a period of consequences.*
—Churchill

Promises

Be cautious in making promises but trustworthy in keeping them.
–Confucius

*Making noble resolutions is not as important as
keeping the promises you have already made.*
–Seneca

Keep your oaths.
–Muhammad

*There is no more lawful debt than the word of a just man, nor
anything that more binds our actions than a promise.*
–Elizabeth

*Resolve to perform what you ought; perform
without fail what you resolve.*
–Franklin

The only safe rule is to promise little, and faithfully to keep every promise.
–Roosevelt

*Never make a promise in haste. Having once made a
promise, fulfill it even at the cost of your life.*
–Gandhi

You must never make a promise which you do not fulfill.
–Churchill

Reason

The good man obeys the voice of reason.
—Aristotle

*Reason is shared by the Gods and men; in them
it is perfected; in us it is perfectible.*
—Seneca

*What is best in man? Reason, which puts him ahead of the
animals and nearer the Gods. Man's other qualities are shared
with plants and animals. One is strong—so are lions. One is
handsome—so are peacocks. One is swift—so are horses.*
—Seneca

Do you possess reason? Then why not use it!
—Marcus Aurelius

May reason triumph everywhere.
—Catherine

*Resort to simple common sense, which is a fairly certain
method for settling a matter satisfactorily.*
—Catherine

Religion

Until you have served men, how can you serve the spirits? Until you understand how to live, how can you understand death?

–Confucius

What do I not teach? Whatever is fascinating to discuss, divides people against each other, but has no bearing on putting an end to suffering.

–Buddha

Our choice to do good or bad actions, not our beliefs, makes us good or bad.

–Aristotle

It is foolish to pray for it when you can obtain it by your own efforts.

–Seneca

Between the good man and the Gods exists a friendship, with virtue as its bond.

–Seneca

God is near you, with you, inside you.

–Seneca

When you pray do not be like the hypocrites, for they love to pray standing in the synagogues and on the street corners to be seen by others.

–Jesus

Watch out for false prophets. They come to you in sheep's clothing, but inwardly are ferocious wolves.

–Jesus

The Sabbath was made for man, not man for the Sabbath.

–Jesus

There is no compulsion in religion.
—Muhammad

*Woe to those who pray but ignore their moral duties;
those who are all show but refuse to help others.*
—Muhammad

Heaven's mandate moves and pervades everything.
—Zhu Xi

Those who appear the most sanctified are the worst.
—Elizabeth

*Serving God is doing good to man, but praying is thought
an easier service, and therefore more generally chosen.*
—Franklin

*If men are so wicked as we see them with religion,
what would they be without it?*
—Franklin

*Sin is not hurtful because it is forbidden, but
it is forbidden because it is hurtful.*
—Franklin

What is serving God? Tis doing good to man.
—Franklin

*We should be very cautious of violating the rights of conscience
in others, ever considering that God alone is judge of the hearts
of men, and to him only in this case are they answerable.*
—Washington

The determinations of Providence are always wise, often inscrutable; and, though its decrees appear to bear hard on us at times, is nevertheless meant for gracious purposes.
—Washington

Mysteries are not necessarily miracles.
—Goethe

Piety is not an end in itself, but a means of attaining tranquility of the soul and the highest values. This is why it is commonly observed that those who proclaim piety as the sole end often turn out to be hypocrites.
—Goethe

We maintain it an outrage, in voting for a man of any position, whether state or national, to take into account his religious faith, provided only he is a good American.
—Roosevelt

I know that one can worship the Creator and dedicate oneself to good living in a grove of trees, or by a running brook, or in one's own house as well as a church. But I also know as a matter of cold fact that the average man does not thus worship or thus dedicate himself.
—Roosevelt

To be just with all men, to be merciful to those to whom mercy should be shown, to realize that there are some things that must always remain a mystery to us, and when the time comes for us to enter the great blackness, to go smiling and unafraid. That is my religion, my faith.
—Roosevelt

We get closer to God as we get more intimately and understandingly acquainted with the things he has created.
—Carver

212

Of course God speaks to you through the things he has created.
—Carver

*Having good wishes for others; doing good deeds for others;
listening to good singing and instrumental music; studying to
master some trade; saying words of good cheer; and above
all doing to others as you wish to be done by—all are part
of how you contact and keep in tune with thy Creator.*
—Carver

*When I admire the wonders of the sunset or the beauty of the
moon, my soul expands in the worship of the creator.*
—Gandhi

*Religions are different roads converging on the same
point. What difference does it make if we follow different
routes, provided we arrive at the same destination?*
—Gandhi

God has no religion.
—Gandhi

*I am not a pillar of the Church but a buttress—I
support it from the outside.*
—Churchill

Reputation

*A gentleman hates the idea of not leaving
behind a good name when he is gone.*
−Confucius

Honor is the prize of virtue that is awarded to good people.
−Aristotle

*I would rather go to any extreme than suffer
anything that is unworthy of my reputation.*
−Elizabeth

Glass, china, and reputation are easily cracked, and never well mended.
−Franklin

A man is really only alive when he delights in the goodwill of others.
−Goethe

The one thing I want to leave my children is an honorable name.
−Roosevelt

*The moment there is suspicion about a person's
motives, everything he does becomes tainted.*
−Gandhi

Self-Reliance

*Superior people make demands on themselves, while
small people make demands on others.*
−Confucius

He who cannot find help within, cannot find help from another.
−Catherine

*The worst lesson that can be taught a man is to rely
upon others and to whine over his sufferings.*
−Roosevelt

*We are the architects of our own fortune and
the hewers of our own destiny.*
−Carver

The threat of adversity is a necessary factor in stimulating self-reliance.
−Churchill

Speaking

Even if your mind is racing, control your mouth.
−Ptah-Hotep

*Silence is better than babbling−but speak when
you know you have the solution.*
−Ptah-Hotep

A good man wants to be slow to speak but quick to act.
−Confucius

*The good man agrees with others without being a mere echo.
The small man echoes without being in agreement.*
−Confucius

*One thoughtful word that brings peace of mind is
better than a thousand meaningless statements.*
−Buddha

One is not wise just because he talks a lot.
−Buddha

We don't need to use many words, but effective ones.
−Seneca

The mouth speaks what the heart is full of.
−Jesus

*Speak what seems most just to you; but speak
kindly, modestly, and without hypocrisy.*
−Marcus Aurelius

Sages never talk to excess.
—Zhu Xi

I see and am silent.
—Elizabeth

Wise men will not speak of a subject that does not pertain to them.
—Elizabeth

Do not tell secrets to those whose faith and
silence you have not already tested.
—Elizabeth

Half-wits speak much but say little.
—Franklin

Silence is not always a sign of wisdom; but babbling is ever of folly.
—Franklin

Let us pay no attention to those overgrown children, who do not
know what they are saying and who talk just for the sake of talking.
—Catherine

Contradiction and flattery both make for poor conversation.
—Goethe

Be generous with kindly words, especially toward those who are absent.
—Goethe

Speak softly and carry a big stick.
—Roosevelt

Speak only if it improves upon the silence.
    −Gandhi

Silence becomes cowardice when occasion demands
speaking out the whole truth and acting accordingly.
    −Gandhi

Teaching

Not to teach a man who may benefit is to let a man go to waste. To try and teach a man who is incapable of benefitting is a waste of your words. A wise man neither lets men nor words go to waste.
—Confucius

Rotten wood cannot be carved.
—Confucius

Men learn as they teach.
—Seneca

If there cannot be money found to answer the common purposes of education, it is evident that there is something amiss in the ruling political power.
—Washington

In universities they teach far too many things and far too much that is useless.
—Goethe

There is no school equal to a decent home, and no teacher equal to a virtuous parent.
—Gandhi

The first duty of a university is to teach wisdom, not a trade; character, not technicalities.
—Churchill

Truthfulness

Doing your best and keeping your word
should be your guiding principle.
−Confucius

A man whose word cannot be trusted is useless.
−Confucius

Conquer the liar with truth.
−Buddha

The person who says what is not true and who
denies what he has done is bound for hell.
−Buddha

Lies are vile and blameworthy while truth is noble and praiseworthy.
−Aristotle

All exaggeration is offensive.
−Aristotle

It is cowardly to hide your feelings and to care less for
the truth than for what people will think of you.
−Aristotle

The good man is guided by the truth.
−Seneca

Prove to me that I am mistaken in word or deed and I will gladly
change—for truth is what I seek and the truth has never harmed
anyone. Harm comes from clinging to error and ignorance.
−Marcus Aurelius

*Truth is invincible. Illusions fail and all disputes
that arise from them become absurd.*
—Catherine

*There is but one straight course; that is to seek
the truth and pursue it steadily.*
—Washington

Wisdom is found only in truth.
—Goethe

It is much easier to recognize error than to find the truth.
—Goethe

*Be truthful—a lie implies fear, vanity, or malevolence; be frank—
furtiveness and insincerity are faults incompatible with true manliness.*
—Roosevelt

The liar is no whit better than the thief.
—Roosevelt

A lady or gentleman is too brave to lie.
—Carver

*An error does not become truth by reason of multiplied propagation,
nor does the truth become error because nobody sees it.*
—Gandhi

*The truth is incontrovertible. Panic may resent it; ignorance
may deride it; malice may destroy it, but there it is.*
—Churchill

No one should swerve off the high road of truth and honor.
—Churchill

Virtue and Character

*Without virtue a man cannot long endure adversity
and cannot long enjoy prosperity.*
−Confucius

*To live virtuously, to have faith, to attain wisdom
and to avoid evil−that is happiness.*
−Buddha

You will have a happy life if you live according to virtue.
−Aristotle

Blessed are the pure in heart.
−Jesus

Wherever life is possible, it is possible to live in virtue.
−Marcus Aurelius

The Way of Heaven blesses the good and harms the wicked.
−Zhu Xi

Virtue and happiness are mother and daughter.
−Franklin

Good moral character is the first essential in a man.
−Washington

Happiness and moral duty are inseparably connected.
−Washington

Character calls forth character.
−Goethe

It is only men of practical ability, knowing their capabilities and using them with moderation and prudence, who will be successful in this world.

—Goethe

Bodily vigor is good, and vigor of intellect is even better, but far above is character.

—Roosevelt

Courage, hard work, self-mastery, and intelligent effort are all essential to successful life.

—Roosevelt

If a man does not have an ideal and try to live up to it, then he becomes a mean, base, and sordid creature, no matter how successful.

—Roosevelt

War and Peace

The sage puts aside weapons and renounces violence toward all creatures.
—Buddha

Wisdom speaks for peace, calling for all mankind to live in harmony.
—Seneca

All who draw the sword will die by the sword.
—Jesus

Blessed are the peacemakers.
—Jesus

If [your enemies] lean toward peace, make peace with them.
—Muhammad

It is a dangerous matter to enter into war.
—Elizabeth

Monarchs ought to put to death the authors and instigators of war, as their sworn enemies and as dangers to their states.
—Elizabeth

There is nothing as good as peace.
—Catherine

When it comes to blows, it is better to deliver them than to receive them.
—Catherine

There is nothing so likely to produce peace as to be well prepared to meet an enemy.
—Washington

The only proper rule is never to fight at all if you can properly avoid it, but never under any circumstances to fight in a half-hearted way.
—Roosevelt

The curse of every ancient civilization was that its men in the end become unable to fight. Each became in the end a nation of pacifists, and then each was trodden under foot by some ruder people that had kept that virile fighting power the lack of which makes all other virtues useless and sometimes even harmful.
—Roosevelt

A nation should never fight unless forced to; but it should always be ready to fight.
—Roosevelt

War with its glorification of brute force is essentially a degrading thing.
—Gandhi

In war, resolution. In defeat, defiance. In victory, magnanimity. In peace, goodwill.
—Churchill

Nothing is more costly and nothing is more sterile than vengeance.
—Churchill

Wealth and Greed

*If you want to behave well and to be free of evil, do not
be greedy. Greed is a fatal and incurable sickness.*

—Ptah-Hotep

*Don't be greedy when it comes to the dividing of
riches, take only what is your fair share.*

—Ptah-Hotep

*Wealth and power are what people want, but if they cannot be
attained in the proper way, you should have no part of them.*

—Confucius

*The good man worries about following the
honorable path, not about poverty.*

—Confucius

*A good man takes as much trouble to discover what is
right as lesser men take to discover what will pay.*

—Confucius

*Wealth harms the greedy, but not those who seek wisdom.
Craving wealth, the fool destroys himself as he does others.*

—Buddha

The greedy do not go to heaven.

—Buddha

Without virtue it is not easy to bear the gifts of good fortune suitably.

—Aristotle

*All things taken to excess bring harm, but unlimited
wealth is the most dangerous of all.*
–Seneca

How hard it is for the rich to enter the kingdom of God.
–Jesus

You cannot serve both God and money.
–Jesus

Be thrifty and frugal: do not spend or consume wildly.
–Zhu Xi

Success has ruined many a man.
–Franklin

Everything in the world may be endured except for continual prosperity.
–Goethe

Prosperity by itself never made any man happy.
–Roosevelt

*No people has ever benefited from riches if their
prosperity corrupted their virtue.*
–Roosevelt

*Too much cannot be said against the men of wealth
who sacrifice everything in getting wealth.*
–Roosevelt

*There are so many people who do not think farther
ahead than the amount of money they can collect.
Sometimes money is the last thing we need.*
−Carver

*History bears witness to the truth that luxury leads to
the destruction and degradation of the nation.*
−Gandhi

Earth provides enough for every man's need but not every man's greed.
−Gandhi

Wealth that is not put to good use is useless.
−Gandhi

Wisdom and Knowledge

To know what you know, and to know what
you do not know—this is wisdom.
−Confucius

The foolish who know they are foolish have a little wisdom.
But fools who look on themselves as wise are fools indeed.
−Buddha

As irrigators lead water to the field, as fletchers shape arrows to fly
straight, as carpenters carve wood, so the wise direct their lives.
−Buddha

The wise man is dearest to the Gods.
−Aristotle

Many people could attain wisdom if they were not
convinced that they had already done so.
−Seneca

Scholars should study every affair under heaven.
−Zhu Xi

Experience keeps a dear school, yet fools will learn from no other.
−Franklin

Without freedom of thought, there can be no such thing as wisdom.
−Franklin

If we cannot learn wisdom from experience, it
is hard to say where it is to be found.
−Washington

The foolish and the wise are equally harmless. It is the half-wise and half-foolish who are the most dangerous.
—Goethe

With knowledge grows doubt.
—Goethe

Nothing is so damaging as ignorance.
—Carver

Look about you. Take hold of the things that are there. Let them talk to you. You talk to them.
—Carver

It is unwise to be too sure of one's wisdom.
—Gandhi

All wisdom is not new wisdom.
—Churchill

Work

Be serious and careful in all you do.
—Confucius

If anything is worth doing, do it with all your heart.
—Buddha

*Every moment be resolved as becomes a Roman and a man to perform
the work at hand with seriousness, goodwill, freedom, and justice.*
—Marcus Aurelius

Do not labor unwillingly, or selfishly, or thoughtlessly, or half-heartedly.
—Marcus Aurelius

The end crowneth the work.
—Elizabeth

When men are employed they are best contented.
—Franklin

*A man who spends his life doing something which he finally
realizes is pointless hates his occupation but cannot change it.*
—Goethe

*Far and away the best prize that life offers is the
chance to work hard at work worth doing.*
—Roosevelt

Do what you can with what you have where you are.
—Roosevelt

Success—real success—does not depend on the position you hold but upon how you carry yourself in that position.
—Roosevelt

Work done willingly and cheerfully is never felt as a burden.
—Gandhi

As long as the job is done, it does not matter much who gets the credit.
—Churchill

It is no use doing what you like; you have got to like what you do.
—Churchill

Work-Life Balance

He that toils all day long has no happy moments, but he who amuses himself all day long cannot provide for his family.
—Ptah-Hotep

Follow your heart as long as you live. Do not work excessively, squandering your opportunities to follow your heart—this is an abomination to your spirit. Don't waste all your time accumulating wealth, for once wealth has been obtained it does no good to someone who is weary and glum.
—Ptah-Hotep

The work first, the reward afterwards.
—Confucius

Too much effort leads to anxiety while too little leads to laziness. Keep your efforts balanced.
—Buddha

Rest and play seem to be necessary for our lives.
—Aristotle

Some people who boast of their foresight and planning are actually the most foolish. They are always preoccupied with work so that they can someday live better; but they consume their lives preparing to live.
—Seneca

The mind must have relaxation; once rested and refreshed it will rise up keener and stronger for new challenges.
—Seneca

When you play, play hard; when you work, don't play at all.
—Roosevelt

*I believe in rough manly sports. But I do not believe in them
if they degenerate into the sole end of one's existence.*
—Roosevelt

There is more to life than increasing its speed.
—Gandhi

Other Maxims

Wretched is he who harms a weak man.
—Ptah-Hotep

Don't make other people fearful, or the Gods will do the same to you.
—Ptah-Hotep

*A good man is calm and at ease, but the small
man is always full of anxiety.*
—Confucius

*The good man helps bring out the best in others,
he does not bring out the worst.*
—Confucius

*A gentleman honors those that excel, but is tolerant of
everyone. He praises the good and pities the incompetent.*
—Confucius

As rust consumes iron, so evil deeds consume those who do them.
—Buddha

*As fresh milk takes time to spoil, so selfish
deeds take time to bring sorrow.*
—Buddha

*Pleasant words and a pretty face are not beautiful if their
owner is jealous, selfish, or deceitful. Only those who have
cast off these flaws are fit to be called beautiful.*
—Buddha

A great man will never or only reluctantly ask for favors, but is always ready to offer them.
—Aristotle

Small men become flatterers.
—Aristotle

Habit is easier to change than nature.
—Aristotle

We have all sinned, some in serious things, some in trifling, some deliberately and some by chance.
—Seneca

Wisdom calls for simple living, not for self-punishment.
—Seneca

The wise man is at home everywhere.
—Seneca

Many men manufacture grievances, either by suspecting what is not true, or by exaggerating the unimportant.
—Seneca

Trusting everyone and trusting no one are equally wrong.
—Seneca

Can any one of you by worrying add a single day to your life?
—Jesus

Do not be wasteful. God does not like wasteful people.
—Muhammad

Be good to your parents. If they reach old age, say no impatient or harsh words, speak to them respectfully, and look after them with kindness.
—Muhammad

Blessed are those who are not miserly or extravagant, but instead spend in moderation.
—Muhammad

Be dutiful to your parents, respect your elders and superiors, be friendly to your birth and marital kin, and be sympathetic to your neighbors.
—Zhu Xi

No good can come from evil.
—Elizabeth

The stone often recoils on the head of the thrower.
—Elizabeth

An investment in knowledge always pays the best interest.
—Franklin

Having been poor is no shame, but being ashamed of it is.
—Franklin

One must live and let others live.
—Catherine

One cannot work at multiple trades at once.
—Catherine

It is easier to admire talents than imitate them.
—Catherine

*It is far better to have no allies than vacillate from one
side to the other like a reed during a storm.*
—Catherine

It is better to offer no excuse than a bad one.
—Washington

There is no practice more dangerous than that of borrowing money.
—Washington

No one is more a slave than the person who falsely thinks he is free.
—Goethe

Nothing is more terrible than ignorance in action.
—Goethe

Everyone only hears what they understand.
—Goethe

One usually considers people more dangerous than they actually are.
—Goethe

*The great point is not to pull down, but to build
up; in this humanity finds pure joy.*
—Goethe

*What would be the use of poets if they only
repeated the record of the historian.*
—Goethe

Much has been given to us, and much will rightfully be expected of us.
—Roosevelt

*Optimism is a good characteristic—but if carried
to excess it becomes foolishness.*
—Roosevelt

There is delight in the hardy life of the open.
—Roosevelt

*I have scant use for the type of sportsman which consists
merely in looking on the feats of someone else.*
—Roosevelt

*It is a good thing to be a good halfback, but it is a mighty bad thing
if at forty all you can say of a man is that he was a good halfback.*
—Roosevelt

*The law can do something, but the law never yet made a
fool wise or a coward brave or a weakling strong.*
—Roosevelt

Selfishness and self are at the bottom of a lot of troubles in the world.
—Carver

Man often becomes what he believes himself to be.
—Gandhi

*I am a lover of my own liberty, and so I
would do nothing to restrict yours.*
—Gandhi

Evils can be created much more quickly than they can be cured.
—Churchill

The power of man has grown in every sphere except over himself.
—Churchill

CONCLUSION:
TEN LAWS FOR A FLOURISHING LIFE

I believe that the most important concepts embodied by the maxims in this book can be condensed into a few simple rules. These natural laws have been perceived by most of the world's great ethical, religious, and philosophical traditions. History has repeatedly shown that following these rules will not only make you a better person, but also a more successful one:

1. Treat all creatures as you would like to be treated.

2. Be honest, truthful, and trustworthy in all things large and small.

3. Be moderate—either extreme is likely to cause harm, unhappiness, or unfairness.

4. Treat others justly according to their deeds and character but also demand equal justice from them.

5. Be physically, intellectually, and emotionally brave.

6. Be happy with your gifts however humble but always strive to improve yourself and your world.

7. Work hard at work worth doing, but don't forget to play hard too.

8. Choose your spouse carefully, have children, and cherish your family; few things are as conducive to a happy life, and nothing is more necessary for a successful society.

9. Choose your friends carefully, but once chosen be steadfast in your friendship.

10. Honor what is sacred in nature, the universe, and in your fellow man; but accept with dignity that some things cannot be known to us.

Thank You for Reading

I hope you found this work to be enlightening, empowering, and enjoyable. Having read the book, please consider sharing an honest review.

REFERENCES

Ptah-Hotep

Gunn, B.G. *The Instruction of Ptah Hotep: And the Instruction of Ke'Gemni*. London: John Murray, 1906.

Horne, C.F. *Sacred Books and Early Literature of the East, Vol. 2: Egypt*. New York: Parke, Austin and Lipscomb, 1917.

Jacq, Christian. *The Wisdom of Ptah-Hotep: Spiritual Treasures from the Age of the Pyramids and the Oldest Book in the World*. London: Constable, 2006.

Lichtheim, Miriam. *Ancient Egyptian Literature, Volume I: The Old and Middle Kingdoms*. Berkeley: University of California Press, 1973.

Shaw, Ian. *The Oxford History of Ancient Egypt*. Oxford: Oxford University Press, 2000.

Confucius

Ames, Roger T. and Henry Rosemont. *The Analects of Confucius: A Philosophical Translation*. New York: Ballantine Books, 1998.

Benjamin, Craig G. *Foundations of Eastern Civilization – Course Guidebook*. Chantilly, Virginia: The Teaching Company, 2013.

Confucius. *The Analects*. Translated by D. C. Lau. London: Penguin Classics, 1979.

Dan, Yu. *Confucius from the Heart*. Translated by Esther Tyldesley. New York: Atria Books, 2006.

Waley, Arthur. *Sacred Writings: Confucianism: The Analects of Confucius*. London: George Allen and Unwin Ltd., 1938.

Buddha

Armstrong, Karen. *Buddha*. New York: Penguin Books, 2001.

Easwaran, Eknath. *The Dhammapada*. Canada: Nilgiri Press, 2010.

Fronsdal, Gil. *The Dhammapada*. Boston and London: Shambhala, 2006.

Kherdian, David. *The Buddha: The Story of an Awakened Life*. Ashland, Oregon: White Cloud Press, 2004.

Kindness, Clarity, and Insight: The Fourteenth Dalai Lama, His Holiness Tenzin Gyatso. Translated and edited by Jeffrey Hopkins and co-edited by Elizabeth Napper. Ithaca, New York: Snow Lion Publications, 2006.

Roebuck, Valerie. *The Dhammapada*. London: Penguin Books, 2010.

Smith, Huston and Phillip Novak. *Buddhism: A Concise Introduction*. New York: Harper Collins, 2003.

Aristotle

Aristotle. *Aristotle's Nicomachean Ethics*. Translated by R.C. Bartlett and S.D. Collins. Chicago: University of Chicago Press, 2011.

Aristotle. *Nicomachean Ethics*. Translated by Terence Irwin. Indianapolis: Hackett Publishing Company, 1999.

Aristotle. *The Nicomachean Ethics*. Translated by F.H. Peters. New York: Barnes and Noble, 2004.

Aristotle. *Parts of Animals*. Translated by A.L. Peck. Cambridge, Massachusetts: Harvard University Press, 1937.

Aristotle. *On the Parts of Animals*. Translated by J. G. Lennox. Oxford: Clarendon Press, 2001.

Chroust, Anton-Hermann. "Estate Planning in Hellenic Antiquity: Aristotle's Last Will and Testament." *Notre Dame Law Review* 45, no. 4 (1970): 629.

Durant, Will. *The Life of Greece.* New York: MJF Books, 1939.

Koterski, Joseph. *The Ethics of Aristotle – Course Guidebook.* Chantilly, Virginia: The Teaching Company, 2010.

Mark, Joshua J. "Aristotle." Ancient History Encyclopedia. May 22, 2019. www.ancient.eu/aristotle/.

Seneca

Basore, J.W. and Lucius Annaeus Seneca. *Moral Essays.* London: Heinemann, 1928.

Clode, Walter. *The Morals of Seneca: A Selection of His Prose.* London: Walter Scott Limited, 1888.

Fantham, Elaine. *Seneca – Selected Letters.* Oxford: Oxford University Press, 2010.

Hadas, Moses. *The Stoic Philosophy of Seneca: Essays and Letters.* New York: Norton and Company, 1958.

Seneca and Tobias Reinhardt. *Dialogues and Essays.* Translated by John Davie. Oxford: Oxford University Press, 2007.

Seneca. *Letters from a Stoic.* Translated by Robin Campbell. London: Penguin Books, 1969.

Jesus of Nazareth

Ehrman, Bart D. *Jesus: Apocalyptic Prophet of the New Millennium.* Oxford: Oxford University Press, 1999.

Jefferson, Thomas. *The Jefferson Bible: The Life and Morals of Jesus of Nazareth.* Bedford, Massachusetts: Applewood Press, 1895.

Tacitus. *The Annals of Imperial Rome.* Translated by Michael Grant. London: Penguin Classics, 1956.

Wilken, Robert Louis. *The Christians as the Romans Saw Them.* New Haven: Yale University Press, 2003.

Marcus Aurelius

Gibbon, Edward. *The Decline and Fall of the Roman Empire.* London: William Strahan, 1776.

Marcus Aurelius. *The Emperor's Handbook.* Translated by C. Scot Hicks and David Hicks. New York: Scribner, 2002.

Marcus Aurelius. *Meditations.* Translated by George Long. New York: Barnes and Noble, 2003.

Marcus Aurelius. *Meditations.* Hollywood, Florida: Simon and Brown, 2011.

Scarre, Chris. *Chronicle of the Roman Emperors.* London: Thames and Hudson, 1995.

Muhammad

Ali, Maulana Muhammad. *A Manual of Hadith.* Lahore, Pakistan: ZuuBooks, 2011.

Al-Qur'an. Translated by Ahmed Ali. Princeton: Princeton University Press, 2001.

Eaton, Charles le Gai. *The Book of Hadith.* Translated by Robson and re-translated by Mahmoud Mostafa. Watsonville, California: The Book Foundation, 2008.

The Koran. Translated by J. M. Rodwell. London: Phoenix, 2001.

The Qur'an. Translated by M.A.S. Abdel Haleem. Oxford: University Press, 2004.

Warner, Bill. *The Sunna of Mohammed.* U.S.A.: Center for the Political Study of Islam, 2010.

Zhu Xi

Adler, Joseph. *Reconstructing the Confucian Dao: Zhu Xi's Appropriation of Zhou Dunyi.* Albany: State University of New York Press, 2014.

Gardner, Daniel. *Zhu Xi's Reading of the Analects: Canon, Commentary and the Classical Tradition.* New York: Columbia University Press, 2003.

Gardner, Daniel. *The Four Books: The Basic Teachings of the Later Confucian Tradition.* Indianapolis: Hackett Publishing Company, 2007.

Ivanhoe, Philip. *Zhu Xi: Selected Writings.* New York: Oxford University Press, 2019.

Jones, David and Jinli He. *Returning to Zhu Xi: Emerging Patterns with the Supreme Polarity.* Albany: State University of New York Press, 2015.

Le Guin, Ursula and Lao Tzu. *Tao Te Ching: A Book about the Way and the Power of the Way.* Boulder: Shambhala Publications, 2019.

Thompson, Kirill. "Zhu Xi." *The Stanford Encyclopedia of Philosophy (Summer 2017 Edition)*, E. N. Zalta (Ed.), https://plato.stanford.edu/archives/sum2017/entries/zhu-xi.

Elizabeth

Chamberlin, Frederick. *The Sayings of Queen Elizabeth.* London: John Lane the Bodley Head Ltd., 1923.

Marcus, L.S., J. Mueller, and M.B. Rose. *Elizabeth I, Collected Works.* Chicago: University of Chicago Press, 2000.

Loades, David. *Elizabeth I.* London and New York: Hambledon and London, 2003.

Milton, Giles. *Big Chief Elizabeth: How England's Adventurers Gambled and Won the New World.* London: Hodder and Stoughton, 2000.

Somerset, Anne. *Elizabeth I.* New York: Anchor Books, 2003.

Franklin

Brands, H.W. *The First American: The Life and Times of Benjamin Franklin.* New York: Anchor Books, 2002.

Franklin, Benjamin. *Wit and Wisdom.* White Plains, New York: Peter Pauper Press, 1962.

Franklin, Benjamin. *Wit and Wisdom from Poor Richard's Almanack.* New York: Dover Publications, 1999.

Franklin, Benjamin. *Quotations of Benjamin Franklin.* Bedford, Massachusetts: Applewood Books, 2003.

Kramnick, Isaac. *The Portable Enlightenment Reader.* New York: Penguin Books, 1995.

Wood, Gordon. *The Americanization of Benjamin Franklin.* New York: The Penguin Press, 2004.

Catherine

Bobrick, Benson. *East of the Sun: The Epic Conquest and Tragic History of Siberia.* New York: Poseidon Press, 1992.

Catherine the Great. *Selected Letters.* Translated by Andrew Kahn and Kelsey Rubin-Detlev. Oxford: Oxford University Press, 2018.

Catherine the Great. *The Grand Instruction to the Commissioners Appointed to Frame a New Code of Laws for the Russian Empire.* Translated to English in London, 1768.

Cruse, Markus and Hilde Hoogenboom. *The Memoirs of Catherine the Great.* New York: Modern Library, 2006.

Massie, Robert. *Catherine the Great: Portrait of a Woman.* United States: Random House, 2012.

Troyat, Henri. *Catherine the Great.* New York: Penguin Group, 1994.

Washington

Chernow, Ron. *Washington, A Life.* New York: Penguin Press, 2010.

Ellis, Joseph J. *His Excellency: George Washington.* New York: Alfred A. Knopf, 2004.

Flexner, James Thomas. *Washington, The Indispensable Man.* New York: Penguin Books, 1969.

McCullough, David. *1776.* New York: Simon and Schuster, 2005.

Washington, George. *Maxims of George Washington.* Edited by John Frederick Schroeder. Mount Vernon, Virginia: The Mount Vernon Ladies Association, 1989.

Washington, George. *Quotations of George Washington.* Bedford, Massachusetts: Applewood Books, 2003.

Goethe

Boerner, Peter. *Goethe.* London: Haus Publishing, 2005.

Durant, Will and Ariel. *The Age of Napoleon.* New York: MJF Books, 1975.

Eckermann, Johann Peter. *Conversations of Goethe.* Translated by John Oxenford. Introduction by Havelock Ellis. United States: Da Capo Press, 1998.

Eckermann, Johann Peter. *Conversations with Goethe.* Revised Edition. Translated by John Oxenford. London: Elibron Classics, 2005.

Goethe, J.W. *Maxims and Reflections.* Translated by Bailey Sanders. London: Macmillan Company, 1906.

Goethe, J.W. *Maxims and Reflections.* Translated by Elisabeth Stopp. Introduction by Peter Hutchinson. London: Penguin Books, 1998.

Jensen, Anthony K. "Johann Wolfgang von Goethe (1749–1832)." Internet Encyclopedia of Philosophy. Accessed September 30, 2020. https://iep.utm.edu/goethe/.

Roosevelt

Egan, Timothy. *The Big Burn: Teddy Roosevelt and the Fire that Saved America.* Boston: Houghton Mifflin Harcourt, 2009.

Hawley, Joshua David. *Theodore Roosevelt: Preacher of Righteousness.* New Haven: Yale University Press, 2008.

Hunt, John Gabriel. *The Essential Theodore Roosevelt.* New York: Gramercy Books, 1994.

Jeffers, H. Paul. *The Bully Pulpit: A Teddy Roosevelt Book of Quotations.* Lanham: Taylor Trade Publishing, 2002.

King, Martin L. "I Have a Dream." Speech presented at the March on Washington for Jobs and Freedom, Washington, D.C., August 1968. http://avalon.law.yale.edu/20th_century/mlk01.asp.

Millard, Candice. *The River of Doubt: Theodore Roosevelt's Darkest Journey.* New York: Anchor Books, 2005.

Morris, Edmund. *The Rise of Theodore Roosevelt.* New York: Ballantine Books, 1980.

Morris, Edmund. *Theodore Rex.* New York: The Modern Library, 2002.

O'Toole, Patricia. *In the Words of Theodore Roosevelt: Quotations from the Man in the Arena.* Ithaca: Cornell University Press, 2012.

Roosevelt, Theodore. *An Autobiography of Theodore Roosevelt.* New York: The Macmillan Company, 1913.

Roosevelt, Theodore. *Quotations of Theodore Roosevelt.* Bedford, Massachusetts: Applewood Books, 2004.

Roosevelt, Theodore. *Theodore Roosevelt's Words of Wit and Wisdom.* New York: Chartwell Books, 2015.

Carver

Burchard, Peter. "George Washington Carver: For His Time and Ours." George Washington Carver National Monument. December 2005. www.nps.gov/gwca/learn/management/upload/GWC-For-His-Time-Ours-Spec-History-Study.pdf.

Federer, William. *George Washington Carver: His Life and Faith in His Own Words.* Saint Louis, Missouri: Amerisearch, 2008.

Hersey, Mark. *My Work Is That of Conservation: An Environmental Biography of George Washington Carver.* Athens, Georgia: University of Georgia Press, 2011.

Kremer, Gary. *George Washington Carver: In His Own Words.* Columbia, Missouri: University of Missouri Press, 1987

McMurry, Linda. *George Washington Carver: Scientist and Symbol.* New York: Oxford University Press, 1981.

Gandhi

Attenborough, Richard. *The Words of Gandhi.* New York: Newmarket Press, 1982.

Calaprice, Alice. *The Ultimate Quotable Einstein.* Princeton: Princeton University Press, 2011.

Easwaran, Eknath. *The Bhagavad Gita.* Canada: Nilgiri Press, 1985.

Fischer, Louis. *The Essential Gandhi.* New York: Vintage Books, 1962.

Gandhi, Mahatma. *The Little Black Book.* California: Renegade Publishing, 2015.

Gandhi, Mahatma. *Quotes of Gandhi.* New Delhi: UBS Publishers, 1984.

Gandhi, Mahatma. *Quotes: Mahatma Gandhi.* California: The Secret Libraries, 2016.

Gandhi, Mahatma. "To Adolf Hitler." Accessed October 5, 2020. Gandhi Book Center. www.mkgandhi.org/mynonviolence/chap60.htm.

James, Lawrence. *The Rise and Fall of the British Empire.* New York: St. Martin's Press, 1994.

Lelyveld, Joseph. *Great Soul.* New York: Vintage Books, 2012.

Mishra, A.D., R. Roa, T. Panakal, and S. R. Tater. *Quotes of Mahatma Gandhi.* Delhi: Abhijeet Publications, 2010.

Sreechinth, C. *So Said Mahatma Gandhi.* California, 2017.

Churchill

Churchill, Winston. *Churchill's Wit: The Definitive Wit of Winston Churchill.* Edited by Richard Langworth. New York: Public Affairs, 2009.

Fromkin, David. *A Peace to End All Peace*. New York: Henry Holt, 1989.

Grunwald, H.A. and Dwight Eisenhower. *Churchill, The Life Triumphant: The Historical Record of Ninety Years*. U.S.A.: American Heritage Magazine and United Press International, 1965.

Johnson, Boris. *The Churchill Factor: How One Man Made History*. New York: Riverhead Books, 2014.

Langworth, Richard. *Churchill by Himself: The Definitive Collection of Quotations*. New York: Public Affairs, 2008.

Manchester, William. *The Last Lion: Winston Spencer Churchill, Alone: 1932–1940*. U.S.A.: Little, Brown and Company, 1988.

Manchester, William. *The Last Lion: Winston Spencer Churchill, Visions of Glory: 1874–1932*. U.S.A.: Little, Brown and Company, 1983.

"The Nobel Prize in Literature 1953." NobelPrize.org. Accessed October 5, 2020. www.nobelprize.org/prizes/literature/1953/summary/.

Multiple

Brinkley, Douglas. *The 100 Most Influential People of all Time. Time Magazine*. New York: Time Books, 2012. (Multiple)

Durant, Will. *Caesar and Christ*. New York: MJF Books, 1944. (Seneca, Jesus, Marcus Aurelius)

Ellis, Joseph J. *Founding Brothers: The Revolutionary Generation*. New York: Vintage Books, 2000. (Franklin, Washington)

Hart, Michael H. *The 100: A Ranking of the Most Influential Persons in History*. New York: Citadel Press, 1994. (Multiple)

Herman, Arthur. *Gandhi and Churchill.* New York: Bantam Dell, 2008. (Gandhi, Churchill)

Melton, Buckner F. Jr. *The Quotable Founding Fathers.* Washington: Potomac Books, 2004. (Franklin, Washington)

Muesse, Mark W. *Confucius, Buddha, Jesus and Muhammad – Course Guidebook.* Chantilly, Virginia: The Teaching Company, 2010. (Confucius, Buddha, Jesus, Muhammad)

Prothero, Stephen. *God is Not One: The Eight Rival Religions that Run the World and Why Their Differences Matter.* New York: HarperOne, 2010. (Confucius, Buddha, Jesus, Muhammad)

Waldman, Steven. *Founding Faith.* New York: Random House, 2008. (Franklin, Washington)

Wright, Esmond. *History of the World: The Last Five Hundred Years.* Middlesex, England: Hamlyn Publishing Group, 1984. (Elizabeth, Catherine)

IMAGE ATTRIBUTION

Ptah-Hotep – Image from similar time period circa 2400 BCE. "Left relief from the tomb of Metjetji" by Rebecca Partington is licensed under CC BY-SA 2.0.

Confucius – Statue of Confucius. "You can't impress #Confucius. #kongfuzi" by James Saper is licensed under CC BY-ND 2.0.

Buddha – Statue of Buddha. "Standing Buddha–Detail 2" by cea+ is licensed under CC BY 2.0.

Aristotle – Bust of Aristotle. "Vienna 014" by Jeremy Thompson is licensed under CC BY 2.0.

Seneca – Bust of Seneca. "Bust of Pseudo-Seneca by Joseph Wilton at The Getty Center in Los Angeles" by Steven Miller is licensed under CC BY 2.0.

Jesus – Icon of Jesus. "Jesus Christ Pantokrator Icon" by Philip K is licensed under CC BY 2.0.

Marcus Aurelius – Bust of Marcus Aurelius. "Marcus Aurelius" by Ed Uthman is licensed under CC BY 2.0.

Muhammad – No image is provided due to the Islamic tradition against visual representations of prophets.

Zhu Xi – Statue of Zhu Xi. "Stock Photo – Zhu Xi Statue" was licensed from 123RF on September 14, 2020.

Elizabeth I – Portrait of Queen Elizabeth attributed to Nicholas Hilliard. "Elizabeth I" by Ann Longmore-Etheridge.

Benjamin Franklin – Bust of Benjamin Franklin. "IMG_3472" by rileydamon is licensed under CC BY-SA 2.0.

Made in United States
Orlando, FL
11 November 2021